GOODMAN'S FIVE-STAR STORIES

After SHOCKS

15 More Startling Stories to Shock and Delight

With Exercises for Comprehension & Enrichment

JAMESTOWN PUBLISHERS

a division of NTC/CONTEMPORARY PUBLISHING GROUP
Lincolnwood, Illinois USA

TITLES IN THE SERIES

After Shocks

Cover and text design: Patricia Volpe, adapted from the original design
by Deborah Hulsey Christie
Cover illustration: Bob Eggleton
Text illustrations: Ann G. Barrow: pp. 47, 48
Heidi Chang: pp. 100–101, 104, 138–139, 142, 144
David Delay: pp. 36–37, 40, 118–119, 122
Maurice P. Dogué: pp. 90–91, 93, 94, 128, 130, 132
Kathleen S. Dwyer: pp. 26, 29, 64–65, 67, 69
Lyn Fletcher: pp. 18–19, 21, 82–83, 85
Timothy C. Jones: pp. 54–55, 74, 77
Pamela R. Levy: pp. 110–111
James Watling: pp. 8, 9, 11, 13

ISBN: 0-89061-751-1

Published by Jamestown Publishers,
a division of NTC/Contemporary Publishing Group, Inc.,
4255 West Touhy Avenue,
Lincolnwood (Chicago), Illinois 60712-1975 U.S.A.

00 01 02 03 04 QB 16 15 14 13 12 11 10 9 8

Contents

To the Student

*T*his book contains 15 exciting stories by some of the world's greatest writers. As the title suggests, each story provides a *shock*. These tales offer you hours of reading pleasure. And the exercises that follow will help you improve your reading and literature skills.

You will notice that the exercises are also based on a *shock:*

SELECTING DETAILS FROM THE STORY

HANDLING STORY ELEMENTS

OBSERVING NEW VOCABULARY WORDS

COMPLETING A CLOZE PASSAGE

KNOWING HOW TO READ CRITICALLY

SELECTING DETAILS FROM THE STORY helps you improve your reading skills.

HANDLING STORY ELEMENTS helps you understand key elements of literature. On page 7 you will find the meanings of ten important terms. If you wish, look back at those meanings when you answer the questions in this section.

OBSERVING NEW VOCABULARY WORDS helps you strengthen your vocabulary skills. Often, you can figure out the meaning of an unfamiliar word by using *context clues* in the story. Those clues are the words and phrases around the unfamiliar word. The vocabulary words in the story are printed in **boldface**. If you wish, look back at these words before you answer the questions in this section.

COMPLETING A CLOZE PASSAGE helps you strengthen your reading *and* your vocabulary skills through the use of fill-in, or cloze, exercises.

KNOWING HOW TO READ CRITICALLY helps you sharpen your critical thinking skills. You will *reason* by using story clues, making inferences (figuring things out), and drawing conclusions.

Another section, **Questions for Writing and Discussion**, gives you opportunities to think, discuss, and write about the stories.

Here is the way to do the exercises:
• There are four questions for each of the SHOCK exercises above.
• Do all the exercises.
• Check your answers with your teacher.
• Use the scoring chart at the end of each exercise to figure out your score for that exercise. Give yourself 5 points for each correct answer. (Since there are four questions, you can get up to 20 points for each exercise.)
• Use the SHOCK scoring chart at the end of the exercises to figure your total score. A perfect score for the five exercises would equal 100 points.
• Keep track of how well you do by writing in your Score Total on the Progress Chart on page 150. Then write your score on the Progress Graph on page 151 to plot your progress.

I know that you will enjoy reading the stories in this book. And the exercises that follow them will help you master some very important skills.

Now . . . get ready for some *After Shocks!*

Burton Goodman

The Short Story—
10 Important Literary Terms

Characterization: how a writer shows what a character is like. The way a character acts, speaks, thinks, and looks *characterizes* that person.

Conflict: a struggle, fight, or difference of opinion between characters.

Dialogue: the words that a character says; the speech between characters.

Main Character: the person the story is mostly about.

Mood: the feeling that the writer creates. For example, the *mood* of a story might be humorous or suspenseful.

Plot: the outline, or order, of events in a story.

Purpose: the reason the author wrote the story. For example, the author's *purpose* might be to amuse the reader.

Setting: where and when the story takes place; the time and place of the action in a story.

Style: the special way that a writer uses language. How a writer arranges words, sentences, and ideas helps to create that writer's *style*.

Theme: the main idea of the story. Note that the *theme* is the central idea of the story. The *plot* is the arrangement, or order, of events.

I

The Jigsaw Puzzle

by Judith Bauer Stamper

*I*t was on the top shelf of an old bookcase, covered with dust and barely visible. Lisa decided she had to find out what it was. Of all the things in the old junk shop, it **aroused** her curiosity most. She had looked through old books, prints, and postcards for hours. But only the old box, high and out of reach, interested her.

She looked around for the old man who ran the store. But he had gone into the back room. She saw a stepladder across the room and brought it over to the bookcase. It shook on the uneven floorboards as she climbed to the top step.

Lisa patted her hand along the surface of the top shelf, trying to find the box. The dirt was thick and gritty on the board. Then she touched the box. It was made of cardboard. The cardboard was cold and soft from being

in the damp room for such a long time. She lifted the box down slowly, trying to steady her balance on the stepladder.

As the side of the box reached her eye level, she could read the words:

500 PIECES

She sat the box down on top of the stepladder and climbed down a few steps. Then she blew away some of the dust on the lid. It billowed up around her with a **stale**, dead odor. But now she could make out a few more words on top of the box:

THE STRANGEST
JIGSAW PUZZLE
IN THE WORLD

There were other words underneath that, but they had been rubbed off the cardboard lid. The big picture on the cover had been curiously damaged. Lisa could make out areas of light and dark. It looked as though the scene might be in a room. But most of the picture had been scratched off the cardboard box, probably by a sharp instrument.

The mysterious nature of the jigsaw puzzle made it even more appealing to Lisa. She decided she would buy it. The lid was taped down securely. That probably meant that all the pieces would be there. As she carefully climbed down the stepladder, holding the box in both hands, Lisa smiled to herself. It was quite a find, just the sort of thing she had always hoped to discover while **rummaging** through secondhand stores.

Mr. Tuborg, the owner of the store, came out of the back room as she was walking up to his sales desk. He looked curiously at the box when Lisa set it down.

"And where did you find that?" he asked her.

Lisa pointed to where she had set up the stepladder. "It was on top of that bookcase. You could barely see it from the floor."

"Well, I've never seen it before, that's for sure," Mr. Tuborg said. "I can't imagine how you found it."

Lisa was more pleased than ever about her find. She felt as though the puzzle had been hiding up there, waiting for her to discover it. She paid

Mr. Tuborg the seventy-five cents he asked for the puzzle and then wrapped it carefully in the newspapers he gave her to take it home in.

It was late on a Saturday afternoon. Lisa lived alone in a small room in an old apartment house. She had no plans for Saturday night. Now she decided to spend the whole evening working on the puzzle. She stopped at a delicatessen and bought some meat, bread, and cheese for sandwiches. She would eat while she put the puzzle together.

As soon as she had climbed the flight of stairs to her room and put away the groceries, Lisa cleaned off the big table in the center of the room. She set the box down on it.

THE STRANGEST
JIGSAW PUZZLE
IN THE WORLD

Lisa read the words again. She wondered what they could mean. How strange could a jigsaw puzzle be?

The tape that held the lid down was still strong. Lisa got out a kitchen knife to slice through it. When she lifted the cover off the box, a damp and dusty smell came from inside. But the jigsaw pieces all looked in good condition. Lisa picked one up. The color was faded, but the picture was clear. She could see the shape of a finger in the piece. It looked like a woman's finger.

Lisa sat down and started to lay out the pieces, top side up, on the large table. As she took them from the box, she sorted out the flat-edged pieces from the inside pieces. Every so often, she would recognize something in one of the pieces. She saw some blonde hair, a window pane, and a small vase. She could see what looked like wallpaper. Lisa noticed that the wallpaper in the puzzle looked a lot like the wallpaper in her own room. She wondered if her wallpaper

11

was as old as the jigsaw puzzle. It would be an amazing coincidence, but it could be the same.

By the time Lisa had all the pieces laid out on the table, it was 6:30. She got up and made herself a sandwich. Already, her back was beginning to hurt a little from leaning over the table. But she couldn't stay away from the puzzle. She went back to the table and set her sandwich down beside her. It was always like that when she did jigsaws. Once she started, she couldn't stop until the puzzle was all put together.

She began to sort out the edge pieces according to their coloring. There were dark brown pieces, whitish pieces, the wallpaper pieces, and some pieces that seemed to be like glass—perhaps a window. As she slowly ate her sandwich, Lisa pieced together the border. When she was finished, she knew she had been right about the setting of the picture when she had first seen the puzzle. It was a room. One side of the border was wallpaper. Lisa decided to fill that in first. She was struck by how much it resembled her own wallpaper.

She gathered together all the pieces that had the blue and lilac flowered design. As she fit the pieces together, it became clear that the wallpaper in the puzzle was exactly the same as the wallpaper in her room. Lisa glanced back and forth between the puzzle and her wall. Yes, it was an exact match.

By now it was 8:30. Lisa leaned back in her chair. Her back was stiff. She looked over at her window. The night was black outside. Lisa got up and walked over to the window. Suddenly, she felt uneasy, alone in the apartment. She pulled the white shade over the window.

She paced around the room once, trying to think of something else she might do rather than finish the puzzle. But nothing else interested her. She went back and sat down at the table.

Next she started to fill in the lower right-hand corner. There was a rug and then a chair. This part of the puzzle was very dark. Lisa noticed uneasily that the chair was the same shape as one sitting in the corner of her room. But the colors didn't seem exactly the same. Her chair was maroon. The one in the puzzle was in the shadows and seemed almost black.

Lisa continued to fill in the border toward the middle. There was more wallpaper to finish on top. The left-hand side did turn out to be a window. Through it hung a half moon in a dark sky. But it was the bottom of the puzzle that began to bother Lisa. As the pieces fell into place, she saw a picture of a pair of legs, crossed underneath a table. They were the legs of a young woman. Lisa reached down and ran her hand along one of her legs. Suddenly, she had felt as though something was crawling on it. But it must have been her imagination.

She stared down at the puzzle. It was almost three quarters done. Only the middle remained. Lisa glanced at the lid to the puzzle box:

THE STRANGEST

JIGSAW . . .

She shuddered.

Lisa leaned back in her chair again. Her back ached. Her neck muscles were tense and strained. She thought about quitting the puzzle. It scared her now.

She stood up and stretched. Then she looked down at the puzzle on the table. Seen from this height, it looked different. Lisa was shocked by what she saw. Her body began to tremble all over.

It was unmistakable—the picture in the puzzle was of her own room. The window was in the same place near the table. The bookcase stood in its exact spot against the wall. Even the carved table legs were the same . . .

Lisa raised her hand to knock the pieces of the puzzle apart. She didn't want to finish the strangest jigsaw puzzle in the world. She didn't want to find out what the hole in the middle of the puzzle might turn out to be.

But then she lowered her hand. Perhaps it was worse not to know. Perhaps it was worse to wait and wonder.

Lisa sank back down into the chair at the table. She fought off the fear that crept into the sore muscles of her back. Slowly and carefully, piece by piece, she began to fill in the hole in the puzzle. She put together a picture of a table, on which lay a jigsaw puzzle. This puzzle inside the puzzle was finished. But Lisa couldn't make out what it showed. She pieced together the young woman who was sitting at the table—the young woman who was herself. As she filled in the picture, her own body slowly filled with horror and dread. It was all there in the picture . . . the vase filled with blue cornflowers, her red sweater, the wild look of fear in her own face.

The jigsaw puzzle lay before her—finished except for two **adjoining** pieces, which fit side by side. They were dark pieces, ones she hadn't been able to fit into the area of the window.

Lisa looked behind her. The white blind was drawn over her window. With relief, she realized that the puzzle picture was not exactly like her room. It showed the black night behind the window pane and a moon shining in the sky.

With trembling hands, Lisa reached for the next to the last piece. She dropped it into one of the empty spaces. It seemed to be half a face, but not a human face. She reached for the last piece. She pressed it into the last small hole left in the picture.

The face was complete—the face in the window. It was more horrible than anything she had ever seen, or dreamed. Lisa looked at the picture of herself in the puzzle and then back to that face.

Then she whirled around. The blind was no longer over her window. The night showed black through the window pane. A half moon hung low in the sky.

Lisa screamed . . . the face—it was there, too!

SELECTING DETAILS FROM THE STORY.
Each of the following sentences helps
you understand the story. Complete each
sentence below by putting an *x* in the
box next to the correct answer.

1. Lisa found the jigsaw puzzle
   - ☐ a. on the top shelf of an old
     bookcase.
   - ☐ b. on a desk in the shop.
   - ☐ c. in the basement of the store.

2. According to Mr. Tuborg, he
   - ☐ a. had many puzzles like the one
     Lisa wanted.
   - ☐ b. knew exactly where Lisa found
     the puzzle.
   - ☐ c. had never seen the box before.

3. The wallpaper in the puzzle was
   - ☐ a. almost the same as the wallpaper
     in Lisa's room.
   - ☐ b. exactly the same as the wallpaper
     in Lisa's room.
   - ☐ c. very different from the wallpaper
     in Lisa's room.

4. Lisa thought that the face in the
   puzzle was
   - ☐ a. quite pleasant.
   - ☐ b. very friendly.
   - ☐ c. horrible to look at.

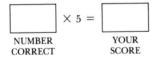

NUMBER
CORRECT

YOUR
SCORE

HANDLING STORY ELEMENTS. Each of
the following questions reviews your
understanding of story elements. Put
an *x* in the box next to the correct
answer to each question.

1. What happened last in the *plot* of
   the story?
   - ☐ a. Lisa paid Mr. Tuborg seventy-
     five cents for the jigsaw puzzle.
   - ☐ b. Lisa noticed a rug and a chair
     in a corner of the puzzle.
   - ☐ c. Lisa saw a face at the window
     of her room.

2. Who is the *main character* in this story?
   - ☐ a. Mr. Tuborg
   - ☐ b. Lisa
   - ☐ c. a strange creature

3. What is the *setting* of the story?
   - ☐ a. a small room in an apartment
     house, one Saturday
   - ☐ b. a large delicatessen, at the
     present time
   - ☐ c. an old book shop, some time in
     the future

4. Which sentence best tells the *theme* of
   the story?
   - ☐ a. You can purchase many
     interesting items in a shop that
     sells old things.
   - ☐ b. Some jigsaw puzzles are very
     difficult to complete.
   - ☐ c. A young woman gets a shock while
     doing a strange jigsaw puzzle.

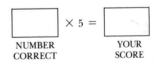

NUMBER
CORRECT

YOUR
SCORE

OBSERVING NEW VOCABULARY WORDS. Answer the following vocabulary questions by putting an *x* in the box next to the correct answer. The vocabulary words are printed in **boldface** in the story. If you wish, look back at the words before you answer the questions.

1. Lisa found the jigsaw puzzle after she had spent hours rummaging through shops. What is the meaning of the word *rummaging*?
   ☐ a. searching
   ☐ b. running
   ☐ c. buying

2. Of all the things in the store, the old box aroused Lisa's curiosity the most. The word *aroused* means
   ☐ a. destroyed or ruined.
   ☐ b. stirred or excited.
   ☐ c. protected or guarded.

3. The box was covered with dust and had a stale, dead odor. Something that is *stale* is
   ☐ a. new.
   ☐ b. very shiny.
   ☐ c. not fresh.

4. The jigsaw puzzle was finished except for two adjoining pieces, which fit side by side. The word *adjoining* means
   ☐ a. next to.
   ☐ b. larger than.
   ☐ c. more expensive than.

COMPLETING A CLOZE PASSAGE. Complete the following paragraph by filling in each blank with one of the words listed in the box below. Each of the words appears in the story. Since there are five words and four blanks, one word in the group will not be used.

The jigsaw is a special kind of saw that contains a _____ , narrow blade. This _____ is excellent for cutting curves and wavy lines. Jigsaws are often used to make the pieces that _____ together in jigsaw puzzles. Therefore, it is easy to see how the jigsaw _____ got its name.

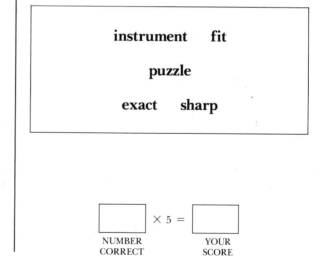

instrument	fit
puzzle	
exact	sharp

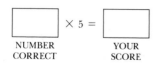

☐ × 5 = ☐
NUMBER CORRECT   YOUR SCORE

☐ × 5 = ☐
NUMBER CORRECT   YOUR SCORE

KNOWING HOW TO READ CRITICALLY. Each of the following questions will help you to think critically about the selection. Put an *x* in the box next to the correct answer.

1. We may infer (figure out) that the face in the window was
   - ☐ a. the face of someone Lisa knew.
   - ☐ b. different from the face in the puzzle.
   - ☐ c. not a human face.

2. In order to feel safer, Lisa
   - ☐ a. told herself that the puzzle wasn't really so strange after all.
   - ☐ b. pulled the shade over the window in her room.
   - ☐ c. decided not to complete the puzzle.

3. Which statement is true?
   - ☐ a. Although the box was dusty and soft, all the pieces of the puzzle were there.
   - ☐ b. Several pieces of the old jigsaw puzzle were missing.
   - ☐ c. The box was in perfect condition, so Lisa could see the picture on its cover very clearly.

4. One amazing thing about the story is that
   - ☐ a. it took Lisa so long to finish a 500-piece puzzle.
   - ☐ b. Lisa paid $7.50 for the puzzle.
   - ☐ c. the picture in the puzzle showed Lisa doing the puzzle.

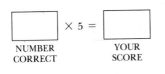

NUMBER CORRECT × 5 = YOUR SCORE

Questions for Writing and Discussion

- The words on the top of the box stated that the puzzle was "The Strangest Jigsaw Puzzle in the World." Was this description correct? Explain your answer.
- When Lisa found the jigsaw puzzle, she was very pleased. She "felt as though the puzzle had been hiding up there, waiting for her to discover it." Do you think the puzzle was meant just for Lisa and for no one else? Give reasons for your answer.
- For a moment, Lisa considered knocking the pieces of the puzzle apart. Should she have done that? Why?

Use the boxes below to total your scores for the exercises. Then write your score on pages 150 and 151.

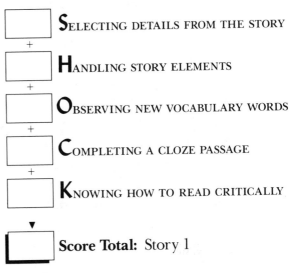

SELECTING DETAILS FROM THE STORY

+

HANDLING STORY ELEMENTS

+

OBSERVING NEW VOCABULARY WORDS

+

COMPLETING A CLOZE PASSAGE

+

KNOWING HOW TO READ CRITICALLY

▼

Score Total: Story 1

2

A Horseman in the Sky

by Ambrose Bierce

One sunny afternoon in the year 1861, a Union soldier lay hidden in a clump of bushes by the side of a road in Virginia. The soldier lay on his stomach with his head on his left arm. His outstretched right hand rested against his rifle. Seeing him so still, one might have thought that he was dead. But the soldier was not dead—he was a scout asleep at his post. However, if he had been discovered sleeping, he would have been as good as dead. For death was the punishment for falling asleep while on duty.

The soldier slept on a winding road which looked over a deep valley. This road zigzagged up to a huge, flat rock which stood at the top of a very high cliff. In fact, a stone dropped from that **gigantic** rock would have fallen a thousand feet to the valley below.

In that valley was a small meadow which ran into a large green forest. And hidden in that forest were five regiments of the Union army.

The regiments had marched all day and all night and were now resting. When night fell, they would march again. They would march to the road and climb, in darkness, to the place where their scout now lay sleeping. From there they would take a path which led behind the enemy's camp. Their hope was to arrive around midnight and to surprise the Confederate troops. But if their plan failed they would be in grave danger, for they were greatly outnumbered. And they would surely fail if the enemy spotted them and saw them moving!

The sleeping soldier was a young Virginian named Carter Druse. He was the son of wealthy parents, and an only child. Druse had known all the ease and comfort which wealth could command in the mountain country of western Virginia. His home was just a few miles from where he now slept. One morning months ago, he had gotten up from the breakfast table and had said quietly but firmly, "Father, a Union regiment has arrived in Virginia. I am going to join it."

The father looked silently at the son for a moment. Then he replied, "Well, go, sir. And whatever may occur, do what you believe to be your duty. You were born in Virginia, and I expected you to join the Confederate forces. Virginia, to which you are a traitor, must get on without you. Should we both live to the end of this war, we will speak of this further. Your mother, as the doctor has **informed** us, is seriously ill. At the most, she cannot be with us much longer than a few weeks. It would be better not to tell her."

So Carter Druse bowed courteously to his father. And with a solemn face that masked a breaking heart, he left to join the Union army.

Druse proved to be a daring and **courageous** soldier. Because of his bravery, as well as his knowledge of the countryside, he had been chosen to serve as a scout. Now, however, **fatigue** had proved stronger than his will. He was exhausted and had fallen asleep.

What caused Carter Druse to awake, who can say? However, he stirred, then quietly lifted his head from his arm. Druse looked around, closing his right hand around the barrel of his rifle as he did. He looked upward and off into the distance.

What he saw was a sight which moved him by its beauty. At the top of the cliff, on a flat rock, was the picture of a man outlined against the sky. He sat quietly on a horse, straight and soldierly. But the man wore the gray uniform of the Confederate army.

The face of the rider was turned slightly away. It showed only the outline of his beard. He was looking downward toward the valley. He was holding a pair of binoculars to his eyes—and he seemed to be staring at something. Framed against the sky, the soldier and the horse suddenly seemed huge to Carter Druse. Druse could not take his eyes off this enemy who seemed so near and so large.

Just then the horse moved its body slightly backward. But the man did not move. Druse brought the butt of his rifle up to his cheek. He pushed the barrel through the bushes and placed his finger on the trigger. He looked through the sights and aimed at a spot on the horseman's chest. A touch of the trigger and all would have been well with Carter Druse. But at that moment the horseman turned his head and looked in the direction of his hidden enemy. The man on the horse seemed to look into Druse's very face, into his eyes, into his heart.

Is it so terrible then to kill an enemy in war—an enemy who has discovered an important secret, an enemy dangerous for what he has learned? Carter Druse grew pale. He began to shake. He grew dizzy and, for a moment, felt his head begin to spin. The rifle dropped to the earth, and suddenly Druse found himself on the ground. This brave soldier came close to fainting, so filled with emotion was he.

But in a moment Druse recovered. In another moment his face was looking upward. His hands found their places on the rifle. His finger reached for the trigger.

Suddenly his mind, heart, and eyes were clear. Druse understood that he could not hope to capture that enemy. And he must stop him from rushing back to camp with the fatal news—that there were Union soldiers in the valley below! Yes, the man must be shot without warning, at once.

But wait, there was a hope. The soldier on horseback might have discovered nothing. Perhaps he was simply admiring the scenery. Certainly the soldier had been staring at something. Druse turned his head and looked downward. He saw, creeping across the green meadow, a thin, winding line of men and horses. Some foolish commander had permitted his soldiers to water their horses in the open. In plain view from the cliff! The man on horseback had certainly seen them.

Druse lifted his eyes from the valley. He stared, again, at the man and the horse against the sky. But this time he stared at them through the sights of his rifle. In his memory rang the words his father had said when they parted: "Whatever may occur, do what you believe to be your duty."

Druse's teeth were set firmly. His breathing became regular and slow as he said to himself, "Peace, be still." He fired.

An officer in the Union army slipped out of the camp in the valley. He had been given an order to look about. He made his way quickly across the meadow and headed toward the road. As he moved, he raised his eyes toward the cliff with its enormous rock. It stood so high above him that it made him dizzy to look up to where it stood against the sky. Peering up to the top of the rock, the officer saw an astonishing sight—a man on horseback riding down into the valley through the air!

The rider sat straight in the saddle, holding tightly to the reins. His long hair streamed upward. The horse seemed to be galloping forward!

The officer was filled with amazement and terror by this ghostly sight of a horseman in the sky. His legs went weak and he fell. At the same moment, he heard a crashing sound in the trees—a sound that died without an echo. Then all was still. Trembling, the officer rose to his feet, looked around and saw nothing. He ran to the spot where he thought he would find the horseman. No one was there. It did not occur to the officer that the horse and its rider would fall directly downward. He could have found them at the bottom of the cliff. But seeing nothing, he returned at once to his camp.

This officer was a wise man. He knew better than to tell a story which no one would believe. He said nothing of what he had seen. Later, the commander asked if he had noted anything of importance. "I saw nothing of interest," the soldier replied.

After firing his shot, Private Carter Druse loaded his rifle and continued his watch. After ten minutes, a Union sergeant crept up to him cautiously on hands and knees.

"Did you fire?" the sergeant whispered.

"Yes."

"At what?"

"A horse. It was standing on that high rock off in the distance. You can see it's no longer there. It went over the edge of the cliff."

Druse's face was pale. Having answered, he turned his eyes away from the sergeant and said no more. The sergeant did not understand.

"See here, Druse," he said, after a moment's silence. "Don't make a mystery of this. I order you to answer. Was there anybody on the horse?"

"Yes."

"Well?"

"My father."

The sergeant rose to his feet and walked away. "Good God!" he said.

SELECTING DETAILS FROM THE STORY.
Each of the following sentences helps
you understand the story. Complete each
sentence below by putting an *x* in the
box next to the correct answer.

1. Carter Druse had been selected to
   serve as
   ☐ a. the commander of the Union
      troops.
   ☐ b. a spy for the Confederate forces.
   ☐ c. a scout.

2. The Union regiments planned to
   ☐ a. attack the Confederate forces
      at daylight.
   ☐ b. surprise the Confederate troops
      around midnight.
   ☐ c. surround the enemy at noon.

3. Druse realized that the solider on
   horseback had
   ☐ a. seen the Union soldiers in the
      meadow below.
   ☐ b. heard several rifle shots.
   ☐ c. noticed him hiding by the side
      of the road.

4. Druse told the sergeant that he had
   fired at
   ☐ a. some Confederate soldiers.
   ☐ b. a traitor.
   ☐ c. a horse.

HANDLING STORY ELEMENTS. Each of
the following questions reviews your
understanding of story elements. Put
an *x* in the box next to the correct
answer to each question.

1. Who is the *main character* in
   "A Horseman in the Sky"?
   ☐ a. Carter Druse
   ☐ b. Druse's father
   ☐ c. the sergeant

2. What happened first in the *plot* of
   the story?
   ☐ a. Druse woke up and saw a soldier
      sitting on a horse.
   ☐ b. The sergeant asked Druse if he
      had fired his rifle.
   ☐ c. The officer was shocked by the
      sight of a horseman riding
      through the sky.

3. The story is *set* in
   ☐ a. the camp of some Confederate
      soldiers.
   ☐ b. a forest where Union soldiers
      were hiding.
   ☐ c. Virginia in 1861.

4. Which sentence best tells the *theme* of
   the story?
   ☐ a. In war, one must always guard
      against a surprise attack.
   ☐ b. A private does his duty as a
      soldier—at a very painful cost.
   ☐ c. A father is surprised when his
      son joins the Union army.

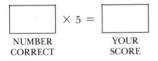

NUMBER
CORRECT

× 5 =

YOUR
SCORE

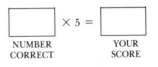

NUMBER
CORRECT

× 5 =

YOUR
SCORE

23

OBSERVING NEW VOCABULARY WORDS.
Answer the following vocabulary questions by putting an *x* in the box next to the correct answer. The vocabulary words are printed in **boldface** in the story. If you wish, look back at the words before you answer the questions.

1. Carter Druse proved to be a daring and courageous soldier. What is the meaning of the word *courageous*?
   □ a. cautious
   □ b. experienced
   □ c. brave

2. A huge rock stood on the top of a very high cliff; a stone dropped from that gigantic rock would have fallen a thousand feet. The word *gigantic* means
   □ a. sharp.
   □ b. enormous.
   □ c. round.

3. Druse was so exhausted that fatigue proved stronger than his will and he fell asleep. The word *fatigue* means
   □ a. tired or weary.
   □ b. showing strength.
   □ c. having knowledge.

4. The doctor informed him that his wife was seriously ill. What is the meaning of the word *informed*?
   □ a. told
   □ b. asked
   □ c. blamed

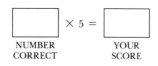

NUMBER CORRECT × 5 = YOUR SCORE

COMPLETING A CLOZE PASSAGE. Complete the following paragraph by filling in each blank with one of the words listed in the box below. Each of the words appears in the story. Since there are five words and four blanks, one word in the group will not be used.

   Four of the first _____ presidents were born in Virginia.

George Washington, Thomas Jefferson, James Madison, and James Monroe all claimed the state of _____ as their home. John Adams, the second president, was _____ in Massachusetts. Interestingly, Adams, Jefferson, and Monroe all _____ on the Fourth of July.

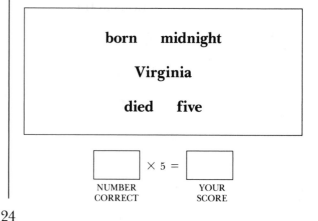

born   midnight

Virginia

died   five

NUMBER CORRECT × 5 = YOUR SCORE

24

KNOWING HOW TO READ CRITICALLY. Each of the following questions will help you to think critically about the selection. Put an *x* in the box next to the correct answer.

1. We may infer (figure out) that the story takes place during
   - ☐ a. the Civil War.
   - ☐ b. World War I.
   - ☐ c. World War II.

2. When Carter Druse announced that he was leaving to join a Union regiment, his father must have been
   - ☐ a. amused by the idea.
   - ☐ b. proud of his son.
   - ☐ c. very disappointed.

3. Why did Druse grow pale and begin to shake when the man on horseback looked in his direction?
   - ☐ a. Druse was afraid that the man was going to fire at him.
   - ☐ b. Druse thought that the man had seen him and was going to ride away.
   - ☐ c. Druse realized that the man on horseback was his father.

4. Druse's words and actions at the end of the story suggest that he was
   - ☐ a. eager to boast about what he had done.
   - ☐ b. upset about what he had done and didn't want to discuss it.
   - ☐ c. planning to run away and return to his home.

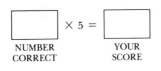

☐ × 5 = ☐

NUMBER   YOUR
CORRECT   SCORE

Questions for Writing and Discussion

- Suppose that Carter Druse's father had *not* told his son, "Whatever may occur, do what you believe to be your duty." Do you think Druse would have acted as he did? Give reasons for your answer.
- With "a solemn face that masked a breaking heart," Druse went off to join the Union army. Describe in detail how Druse felt when he left his home.
- Why did the Union officer think that he had seen a man on horseback riding through the air? What did he actually see? Explain.

Use the boxes below to total your scores for the exercises. Then write your score on pages 150 and 151.

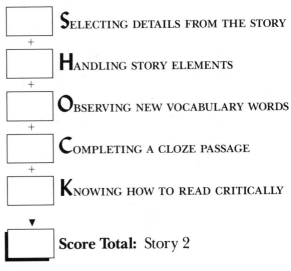

☐   SELECTING DETAILS FROM THE STORY

+

☐   HANDLING STORY ELEMENTS

+

☐   OBSERVING NEW VOCABULARY WORDS

+

☐   COMPLETING A CLOZE PASSAGE

+

☐   KNOWING HOW TO READ CRITICALLY

▼

☐   **Score Total:** Story 2

3

The Eyes Have It

by James McKimmey

*J*oseph Heidel looked slowly around the dinner table at the five Council members who were watching him carefully. Heidel was a large man with thick, graying hair cut close to his head. He was the President of the Superior Council, the most important office on the occupied planet of Mars. He had held that position for the six years he had lived there.

Heidel's bright, narrow eyes flicked from one face to another. As they did, his fingers slowly tapped the tabletop, making a sound like a **miniature** drum roll.

One. Two. Three. Four. Five. He was looking at the five top officials, the five people who had been screened and selected on Earth, to take charge of the government on Mars.

But one of the five was a spy, an impostor. But which one? *Who* was the impostor?

Heidel's fingers continued tapping. Who was the Martian? Which one of the five had not come from Earth?

Marianne Sadler's voice suddenly cut through the silence in the room. "Then this is not just an ordinary meeting, Mr. President?"

Heidel stared into Sadler's eyes. "No, it isn't," he replied. "This is a very special meeting." He grinned. "This is where we gather the sheep to find the wolf."

Heidel watched the five faces. Sadler. Mendez, Locke, Forbes, Clarke. One of them. Which one was the Martian?

"Find the wolf?" said Harry Locke, slowly. "I don't follow what you mean."

"No, no, of course not," Heidel said, still grinning. "Let me explain."

He bent forward, and the words rolled out smoothly. "Here's the story, briefly and simply. We have an impostor among us, an *impostor*—a spy."

Heidel paused, letting his words sink in. This was the kind of situation he liked best, a tense situation, one filled with suspense. Heidel leaned back. "And tonight," he said slowly, "I am going to expose this impostor. Right here, at this table."

He stared at the faces again, searching for the telltale **twitch** of a muscle, the nervous movement of a hand, the worried look in an eye.

But he saw only Sadler, Mendez, Locke, Forbes, and Clarke, looking as they always did, interested, thoughtful, polite.

"One of us, you say?" Elena Clarke said, quietly.

"That's right," replied Heidel.

"Quite a situation," said Frank Forbes, a faint smile on his face. "Quite a situation, indeed."

Eduardo Mendez cleared his throat. "May I ask how this was discovered? And how do you know that the spy is a member of the Superior Council?"

"Of course," Heidel said. "There's no need to go into the troubles we've been having. You know all about that. But how these troubles started is the important thing. You remember the sixty-seven people we **smuggled** here from Earth?"

"The teachers you mean? When we were planning to secretly change the entire education system?"

"That's right," said Heidel, **recalling** it grimly. "All sixty-seven people were killed."

"It was terrible," shuddered Locke.

"I remember the Martian note of apology," said Forbes. *"We have taught our children our way for two-hundred thousand years. We prefer to continue doing it our way."*

"But we were only trying to help them," said Sadler.

"That's neither here nor there," said Heidel. "The important thing is this. No one *knew* about the mission of those sixty-seven men and women. No one, that is, except myself and you five."

Heidel watched the faces in front of him. "There's no point," he said, "in going into the other incidents. You remember them all. You remember how each one of our plans—plans to help these Martians benefit from our culture—was cut off in the bud. Only a leak in the Superior Council could have caused that."

Heidel's voice was suddenly a powerful, low sound that echoed through the dining room. "Yes, one of us here is the person responsible. And I am going to find that person!"

The five people waited. Forbes, his long arms crossed. Clarke, her eyes on the table. Mendez, blinking slowly. Sadler, twirling her thumbs. Locke, his eyes on his fingernails.

"Kessit!" Heidel called.

A gray-haired man in a black butler's coat appeared.

"We'll have our coffee now," said Heidel. He turned back toward the group. "This is a special blend which you'll find quite tasty."

Slowly the butler moved from place to place, pouring coffee from a silver urn.

"Now then, Kessit," Heidel said, "would you be kind enough to fetch me my little pistol from the drawer over there?"

Heidel took the gun from the butler's hand and said, "One thing more, Kessit. Please light the candles on the table. Then turn off the rest of the lights in the room." Heidel smiled. "Now isn't this nice," he said. "Candlelight with our coffee."

"Oh, excellent," said Locke, without enthusiasm.

"Great," said Forbes.

Heidel waited while Kessit lit

the candles and snapped off the overhead lights. The yellow flames flickered over the table as the door closed gently behind the butler.

As soon as Kessit was gone, Heidel held up the pistol so that the candle-light reflected against the handle and the barrel.

"This," he said, "is an antique of the twentieth century—but one which still works."

The five people leaned forward to look at the gun in Heidel's hand.

"Crude," Mendez said.

"But dangerous looking," Sadler added.

"Yes," said Heidel. "And I am quite skillful at using it."

"Well that should be fun," said Forbes, without looking amused.

"The fun begins," said Heidel, "when I discover the Martian in this group!" And he brought the glistening pistol down against the table with a crash.

There was dead silence and then Heidel smiled again. "Now let me explain a bit. You know that Dr. Kingly, the head of our laboratory, died a few days ago. But before he died, he made an amazing discovery. As you know, Earth people and Martians look exactly the same. So there has never been any way—any physical way, at least—to tell a Martian from an Earth person. At least not until Dr. Kingly made his discovery."

Heidel paused. "When I finish my coffee, I'll tell you how it happened." He raised the cup to his lips and watched while the five Council members sipped their coffee in silence.

"Now, then," he went on, "it was while Dr. Kingly was examining the body of a dead Martian that he made his startling discovery."

"I beg your pardon," Forbes said. "Do you mean an autopsy?"

"Yes," said Heidel. "We've done them from time to time. That's against Martian Law, I know, but necessary now and then."

"I see," said Forbes. "I just didn't know about that."

"No, you didn't, did you?" said Heidel, looking closely at Forbes.

"Anyway, Dr. Kingly had developed a solution which he used to preserve the body's tissues. During the examination, he injected the solution into the body. Then he left the Martian on the examining table. When he returned to the laboratory it was night. The laboratory was dark. And before Dr. Kingly switched on the lights, he saw the eyes of this dead Martian. They were *glowing* in the dark like a pair of hot coals!"

"Weird," said Sadler.

"Strange," said Clarke.

"The important thing," Heidel said sharply, "is that Dr. Kingly discovered the difference between Martians and Earth people. The difference *is in the eyes*. It has something to do with the chemicals there."

Heidel's gaze moved slowly from face to face. "At any rate," he continued, "Dr. Kingly's solution causes a Martian's eyes to glow like electric lights. But it has no effect on the eyes of a person from Earth!"

Heidel picked up the pistol from the table. "As you know, I am quite skillful with this weapon. In fact, I am an expert shot. Now I am going to shoot out each of the four candles on this table. Do you all follow me? Locke? Sadler? Mendez? Forbes? Clarke?"

Heads nodded.

"When the last candle has been put out, we will be in darkness. And then we'll find our Martian spy."

Heidel nodded. "Because, you see," he said very slowly, "I have added some of Dr. Kingly's solution to the coffee we have been drinking. Yes, Dr. Kingly's solution! It has no taste and no harmful effects—except to one person in this room."

Heidel raised the gun. "I have five bullets in this pistol. Four for the candles—and one for the Martian whose eyes *will glow in the dark* when the last candle goes out!"

There was silence while the flames of the four candles flickered in the still air in the room.

"Watch carefully," Heidel said, aiming the pistol. The explosion was loud in the room as his finger pulled the trigger.

"One!" said Heidel, as the candle went out.

He aimed again. The explosion echoed.

"Two!" he said. "Rather good firing, wouldn't you agree?"

"Oh, yes," Sadler said.

"Quite," said Forbes.

"Three!" Heidel said. The shot sounded and the third candle went out.

"Now," said Heidel, pointing the pistol at the last candle, "I would say this is it, wouldn't you agree? As soon as this candle goes out, we'll find our Martian."

Heidel squinted one eye and squeezed the trigger. The room echoed and there was blackness. Heidel held his pistol over the table.

Silence. Broken by the gasp of shock which came from Heidel's lips.

"Well, there you have it," said Forbes, finally. "Surprised?"

Heidel clung to the pistol, as his hands went clammy and cold. Staring at him were—*five pairs of glowing eyes!*

"Yes," said Sadler. "*All* of us were in it."

Heidel bit his lips. "How? How did you do it?"

"Simple, really," said Locke. Just put some Martians in place of colonists going back to Earth. Let them study and learn. Then switch some records here, some photographs there. Fairly easy to do. Communication between Mars and Earth isn't that good, you know."

"But why? *Why?*" asked Heidel. "We were planning to give you the *best* of our civilization, the *best* of our culture."

"Perhaps we didn't care for the wrestlers on your TV shows," said Mendez, dryly.

Heidel's nostrils twitched. "Still, I'll get one of you!" he cried, his finger on the trigger.

"Possibly," said Forbes. "Perhaps not. We each have a gun pointed at you. And we can see *you* perfectly, as though it were daylight. The slightest movement of that pistol, and you're gone."

A thought suddenly occurred to Heidel. "Kessit!" he shouted. "Kessit! Sound the alarm! Quickly, send for help!"

"I'm afraid I can't do that, sir," said the butler, at his side. "You see, I too am able to see in the dark."

SELECTING DETAILS FROM THE STORY.
Each of the following sentences helps
you understand the story. Complete each
sentence below by putting an *x* in the
box next to the correct answer.

1. Joseph Heidel was attempting to
   - ☐ a. start a war with the Martians.
   - ☐ b. figure out how to get back to
       Earth.
   - ☐ c. find the Martian spy.

2. The plans of the Superior Council had
   failed because of
   - ☐ a. a leak in the Council.
   - ☐ b. a lack of information about the
       Martians.
   - ☐ c. back luck and bad timing.

3. Dr. Kingly's solution caused a Martian's
   eyes to
   - ☐ a. close.
   - ☐ b. glow brightly.
   - ☐ c. fill with tears.

4. When the last candle went out,
   Heidel saw
   - ☐ a. the body of a dead Martian.
   - ☐ b. several guns pointed at him.
   - ☐ c. five pairs of glowing eyes.

HANDLING STORY ELEMENTS. Each of
the following questions reviews your
understanding of story elements. Put
an *x* in the box next to the correct
answer to each question.

1. What happened last in the *plot* of
   the story?
   - ☐ a. Heidel shot out the first candle.
   - ☐ b. Heidel shouted to Kessit, "Send
       for help!"
   - ☐ c. The butler moved from place to
       place, pouring coffee.

2. "The Eyes Have It" is *set*
   - ☐ a. in the past.
   - ☐ b. in the future.
   - ☐ c. at the present time.

3. "You see, I too am able to see in
   the dark." This line of *dialogue* was
   spoken by
   - ☐ a. Elena Clarke.
   - ☐ b. Joseph Heidel.
   - ☐ c. Kessit, the butler.

4. Because of the author's *style* of writing,
   "The Eyes Have It" may be described
   as a
   - ☐ a. ghost story.
   - ☐ b. love story.
   - ☐ c. science fiction tale.

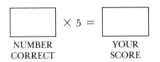

☐ × 5 = ☐

NUMBER   YOUR
CORRECT   SCORE

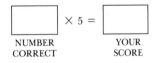

☐ × 5 = ☐

NUMBER   YOUR
CORRECT   SCORE

OBSERVING NEW VOCABULARY WORDS. Answer the following vocabulary questions by putting an *x* in the box next to the correct answer. The vocabulary words are printed in **boldface** in the story. If you wish, look back at the words before you answer the questions.

1. Heidel thought about the disaster, recalling it grimly. What is the meaning of the word *recalling*?
   □ a. remembering
   □ b. causing
   □ c. learning

2. Somehow, the Martians found out about the sixty-seven people who were smuggled there from Earth. The word *smuggled* means
   □ a. tossed away.
   □ b. brought in secretly.
   □ c. questioned for a long time.

3. Heidel's fingers slowly tapped the table-top, making a sound like a miniature drum roll. As used here, the word *miniature* means
   □ a. foolish.
   □ b. smashed.
   □ c. small.

4. He was searching for the twitch of a muscle, the nervous movement of a hand. The word *twitch* means a
   □ a. sudden shaking.
   □ b. great power.
   □ c. weakness.

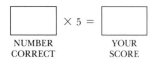

NUMBER CORRECT   YOUR SCORE

COMPLETING A CLOZE PASSAGE. Complete the following paragraph by filling in each blank with one of the words listed in the box below. Each of the words appears in the story. Since there are five words and four blanks, one word in the group will not be used.

Because it has extremely

_____ eyes, the owl looks
    1

wiser than other animals. An owl's eyes

appear to be bigger than they actually

are because they are set in front of the

head, facing _____. An owl
             2

cannot move its _____ from
              3

side to side. To _____ a moving
              4

object, it must turn its head.

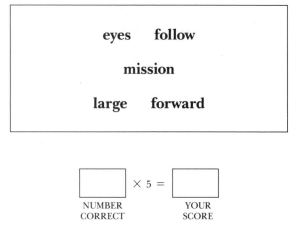

eyes   **follow**

mission

large   **forward**

NUMBER CORRECT   YOUR SCORE

KNOWING HOW TO READ CRITICALLY. Each of the following questions will help you to think critically about the selection. Put an *x* in the box next to the correct answer.

1. After Heidel shot out the last candle, he expected to see
   ☐ a. a pair of glowing eyes.
   ☐ b. the butler at his side.
   ☐ c. five pairs of glowing eyes.

2. Which statement is true?
   ☐ a. At the end of the story, Heidel shot one of the Council members.
   ☐ b. Dr. Kingly's solution didn't really work.
   ☐ c. Except for Heidel, all of the people in the room were Martians.

3. Clues in the story suggest that the people of Mars
   ☐ a. appreciated Heidel's efforts to help them.
   ☐ b. didn't like their system of education.
   ☐ c. didn't think very much of the culture on Earth.

4. The last line of the story indicates that Kessit
   ☐ a. hated his job.
   ☐ b. was a Martian.
   ☐ c. was going to help Heidel.

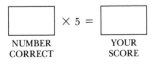

NUMBER CORRECT × 5 = YOUR SCORE

Questions for Writing and Discussion

- In "The Eyes Have It," the Earth people and the Martians "look exactly the same." Explain why that fact is so important to the story.
- Heidel served the Council members a "special blend" of coffee. In what way was the coffee "special"? Why did Heidel pause to watch the Council members drink their coffee?
- In voting, the word *aye* (pronounced *eye*) means "yes." When there are more "yes" votes than "no" votes, one says "The ayes have it." With that in mind, explain the title of the story. Do you think it is a good title? Why?

Use the boxes below to total your scores for the exercises. Then write your score on pages 150 and 151.

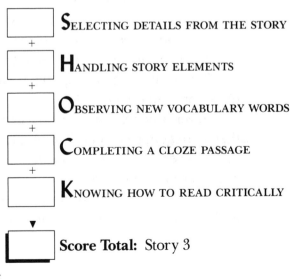

SELECTING DETAILS FROM THE STORY

+

HANDLING STORY ELEMENTS

+

OBSERVING NEW VOCABULARY WORDS

+

COMPLETING A CLOZE PASSAGE

+

KNOWING HOW TO READ CRITICALLY

▼

Score Total: Story 3

4

The Bus

by Shirley Jackson

Miss Harper was going home, although the night was wet and **nasty**. She did not like traveling on this dirty, small bus.

But tonight Miss Harper had no choice. If she missed this bus, she could not go for another day. Miss Harper was tired and angry. She tapped loudly on the ticket counter.

I just can't make this trip again, Miss Harper thought. They really try to make you uncomfortable.

"Can I get my ticket, please?" she said sharply.

"You got three minutes before the bus leaves," the ticket man said.

He'd love to tell me I missed it, Miss Harper thought.

The rain was pouring down. She hurried to the door of the bus. The driver opened the door slowly.

Several people were sitting in the bus. Miss Harper wondered where they were going. Could other people really stand this kind of trip?

I'm very upset, Miss Harper thought. I need to get home. She wanted a hot bath and a cup of tea.

No one helped Miss Harper put her suitcase on the rack. She looked at the driver. He was sitting with his back turned.

Miss Harper had taken a sleeping pill before getting on the bus. She hoped to sleep through most of the trip.

Miss Harper slept poorly until the bus driver woke her up.

"Look, lady," the driver said. He was shaking her. "I'm not an alarm clock. Wake up and get off the bus."

"What?" Miss Harper opened her eyes. She reached for her purse.

"I'm not an alarm clock," the driver repeated. "Get off the bus."

"What?" Miss Harper said again.

"This is as far as you go. You got a ticket to here. You've arrived. It's not my job to carry you off the bus."

"I'm going to report you," Miss Harper said. She was awake now. She straightened her hat.

Without help, Miss Harper took down her suitcase. She struggled with it. The suitcase banged against the seats.

Miss Harper knew people were staring at her. She was afraid she might fall.

"I'm going to report you," Miss Harper told the driver.

"Come on, lady," he said. "It's the middle of the night. I got a bus to run."

"You should be ashamed of yourself," Miss Harper said, wanting to cry.

The door was open. Miss Harper stepped onto the ground. The bus started with a jerk, throwing her backward.

I'll report him, she thought. I'll see that he loses his job. And then she realized she was in the wrong place.

It was dark and rainy. Miss Harper knew she was not in her own town. There were no stores, no lights, no people. There was nothing but a wet road and a signpost.

Don't be frightened, Miss Harper told herself. It's all right. You'll soon see that it's all right.

There was no shelter in sight, but the signpost said RICKET'S LANDING.

So that's where I am, Miss Harper thought. I've come to Ricket's Landing and I don't like it here.

She set her suitcase down. Miss Harper was crying a little.

"Please—won't someone help me?" she asked.

Finally Miss Harper saw headlights. She ran to the middle of the road.

The lights belonged to a small truck. It stopped beside her.

A young man spoke angrily. "You trying to get killed?"

"Please," Miss Harper said. "Please help me. The bus put me off here. It wasn't my stop. I'm lost."

"Lost?" The young man laughed. The driver laughed, too.

"Can you take me somewhere?" Miss Harper asked. "A bus station?"

"No bus station." The young man shook his head. "Bus only comes through here once a night."

"Please," she said. "Can I get in with you, out of the rain?"

The two young men looked at each other. "Take her down to the old lady's," one of them said.

"She's pretty wet to get in the truck," the other one said.

"Please," Miss Harper said. "I'll be glad to pay you what I can."

"We'll take you to the old lady," the driver said.

The driver started the truck. It moved slowly through the mud and rain. What is happening to me? Miss Harper wondered.

"We're going down to the old lady's," the driver said. "She'll know what to do."

"I just want to get home," Miss Harper said.

The truck seat was very **uncomfortable**. She felt clammy and sticky and chilled. Home seemed so far away.

Ahead of them a light blinked. The driver pointed.

"There," he said. "That's where we're going."

They drove closer. Miss Harper was upset. The light belonged to a road-house! Miss Harper had never been in a roadhouse. The sign read:

BEER!

Bar & Grill

"Is there anywhere else I could go?" she asked. "I'm not sure—"

"Not many people here tonight," the driver said.

He pulled into the parking lot. Miss Harper was sad to see that the lot was once a garden.

Miss Harper suddenly felt she recognized the house. It was a lovely place. It had been an old mansion once.

"Why?" Miss Harper asked, wanting to know why this lovely old house had become a Bar & Grill.

The driver **ignored** her. "Get her suitcase," he told the other young man.

Miss Harper followed the men into the old house.

"I used to live in a house like this," she told them.

"I bet you did," one of them said.

Miss Harper stopped. She had just entered a large, dirty room. There was a counter running along one side. In the center were six old tables. A jukebox played in one corner.

"Oh, no," Miss Harper said. She was thinking of how the house must have looked once.

A dozen young people sat around the tables. They all looked alike. They all talked and laughed flatly.

---

1. **roadhouse:** an inn or restaurant located at the side of a road in the country.

Miss Harper thought they were
laughing about her. She was wet and unhappy.
These noisy people did not belong here.

"Come and meet the old lady," the driver said.

Miss Harper followed the two young men to the counter. Her suitcase bumped against her legs. I must be careful not to fall down, she thought.

"Belle, Belle," the driver said. "Look at the stray cat we found."

A huge woman looked Miss Harper up and down.

"You don't say," the woman said at last. "You don't say."

"Please," Miss Harper said. "They put me off my bus at the wrong stop."

"You don't say," the woman said, and laughed. "She sure is wet."

"You'll take care of her?" the driver asked.

Miss Harper was looking for her wallet. How much? she was wondering. It was such a short ride. But if they hadn't come. . . .

She took two $5 bills from her wallet. They can't argue over $5 each, she thought. "Thanks," the driver said.

I could have gotten away with a dollar each, Miss Harper thought.

"Hey, thanks," the other young man said.

"Thank *you*," Miss Harper said.

"I'll put you up for the night," the woman said. "You can sleep here. It'll cost you $10."

She's leaving me bus fare home, Miss Harper thought. She took out her wallet again.

The woman accepted the $10. "Upstairs," she said. "Take your choice. No one's around."

"Thank you." Miss Harper knew where the staircase would be. She went to what had once been the front hall. And there was the staircase. It was so lovely that she caught her breath.

She turned back. The large woman was staring at her.

"I used to live in a house like this," Miss Harper said.

"You don't say," the woman said. She turned back to the counter.

Miss Harper climbed the stairs. She went to the front room on the left. It had always been her room.

The door was open, and she glanced in. The room was ugly and cheap.

Miss Harper turned on the light. She stood in the doorway. The peeling wallpaper made her sad. What have they done to the house? she thought. How can I sleep here tonight?

Miss Harper entered the room and set her suitcase on the bed. I must get dry, she told herself. I must make the best of things.

The bed was correctly placed between the two front windows, but the mattress was lumpy. Miss Harper was frightened by the noisy springs.

I will not think about things, Miss Harper thought. This might be the room I slept in as a girl. There must be 1,000 houses built exactly like this.

The closet, however, was on the wrong side. The big closet had once been her playhouse.

The bathroom was wrong, too. Miss Harper wanted a hot bath before bed. But the dirty bathtub **discouraged** her. She washed her face and hands, and the warm water comforted her.

She was also comforted to find that nothing inside her suitcase was wet. At least she could sleep in a dry nightgown.

Miss Harper shivered in the cold sheets. She lay in the darkness with her eyes open. What was to become of her?

She could hear the jukebox music downstairs. My mother is singing, she thought, and our company is listening. My father is playing the piano.

I could creep to the top of the stairs and listen, she told herself. But then she heard a rustling in the closet. It is more a rattling than a rustling, Miss Harper thought.

The rattling continued. It was just loud enough to bother her. Miss Harper knew she would never sleep until it stopped. She swung her legs over the side of the bed, and walked barefoot to the closet door.

"What are you doing in there?" she asked, and opened the door.

There was just enough light for her to see the wooden snake. Its head was lifted. It rattled itself against the other toys.

Miss Harper laughed. "It's my old snake," she said. "It's come alive."

She could also see her old toy clown, bright and cheerful. He flopped back and forth.

Miss Harper saw a beautiful doll sitting on a chair, with golden curls and wide blue eyes.

Miss Harper held out her hands in joy. The doll opened her eyes and stood up.

"Rosabelle," Miss Harper said. "Rosabelle, it's me."

The doll turned. The red lips opened. The doll said, "Go away, old lady. Go away, old lady. Go away."

Miss Harper backed away. She slammed the closet door and leaned against it. The doll's voice went on and on.

Miss Harper turned and ran. "Mommy," she screamed. "Mommy, Mommy!"

She ran out the door, to the staircase. "Mommy," she cried. Miss Harper fell. She went down and down into darkness. She kept trying to catch onto something real. . . .

"Look, lady," the bus driver was saying. "I'm not an alarm clock. Wake up and get off the bus."

"I am going to report you," Miss Harper said. She wanted to cry.

"This is as far as you go," the driver said.

The bus jerked forward. Miss Harper nearly fell in the pouring rain. Her suitcase was near her feet, under the sign that read RICKET'S LANDING.

SELECTING DETAILS FROM THE STORY.
Each of the following sentences helps
you understand the story. Complete each
sentence below by putting an *x* in the
box next to the correct answer.

1. Although the bus was small and dirty,
   Miss Harper decided to take it because
   - ☐ a. the price of the ticket was so low.
   - ☐ b. the bus driver was so helpful.
   - ☐ c. if she didn't, she would have
     to wait another day.

2. At the roadhouse, Miss Harper picked
   a room that
   - ☐ a. had just been painted.
   - ☐ b. had brightly colored wallpaper.
   - ☐ c. was like the room she had slept
     in as a girl.

3. The doll told Miss Harper to
   - ☐ a. go away.
   - ☐ b. comb its hair.
   - ☐ c. close the closet door.

4. At the end of the story, Miss Harper
   discovered that she was
   - ☐ a. in her own town.
   - ☐ b. at Ricket's Landing.
   - ☐ c. back at the bus station.

HANDLING STORY ELEMENTS. Each of
the following questions reviews your
understanding of story elements. Put
an *x* in the box next to the correct
answer to each question.

1. What happened first in the *plot* of
   "The Bus"?
   - ☐ a. Miss Harper looked in the closet
     and saw her old snake.
   - ☐ b. Miss Harper rented a room for
     ten dollars.
   - ☐ c. Miss Harper purchased a ticket
     and hurried to the bus.

2. Which sentence best *characterizes*
   Miss Harper?
   - ☐ a. She was calm and relaxed at
     all times.
   - ☐ b. She seemed nervous and upset.
   - ☐ c. She was charming and made
     friends very easily.

3. The *mood* of "The Bus" is
   - ☐ a. humorous and amusing.
   - ☐ b. serious and scary.
   - ☐ c. happy or joyous.

4. Which sentence best tells the *theme* of
   the story?
   - ☐ a. A bus driver treats one of his
     passengers rudely.
   - ☐ b. You can't tell what to expect when
     you visit a strange town.
   - ☐ c. A woman has a frightening
     dream—which may be happening
     all over.

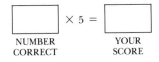

NUMBER
CORRECT   × 5 =   YOUR
                    SCORE

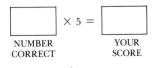

NUMBER
CORRECT   × 5 =   YOUR
                    SCORE

43

OBSERVING NEW VOCABULARY WORDS.
Answer the following vocabulary questions by putting an *x* in the box next to the correct answer. The vocabulary words are printed in **boldface** in the story. If you wish, look back at the words before you answer the questions.

1. Miss Harper decided to go home, although the night was wet and nasty. The word *nasty* means
   ☐ a. delightful.
   ☐ b. clear.
   ☐ c. not pleasant.

2. When Miss Harper asked the driver a question, he ignored her and spoke, instead, to the other man. The word *ignored* means
   ☐ a. paid no attention to.
   ☐ b. offered thanks.
   ☐ c. answered promptly.

3. The truck seat was uncomfortable and Miss Harper felt sticky and chilled. What is the meaning of the word *uncomfortable?*
   ☐ a. satisfied
   ☐ b. confident
   ☐ c. ill at ease

4. Miss Harper wanted to take a bath, but the dirty bathtub discouraged her. As used here, the word *discouraged* means
   ☐ a. encouraged.
   ☐ b. prevented.
   ☐ c. weakened.

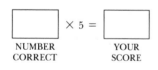

NUMBER CORRECT × 5 = YOUR SCORE

COMPLETING A CLOZE PASSAGE. Complete the following paragraph by filling in each blank with one of the words listed in the box below. Each of the words appears in the story. Since there are five words and four blanks, one word in the group will not be used.

Some _____ claim that
              1

they never dream. But recent studies

suggest that everyone dreams, usually

_____ times a night. Many
          2

people cannot remember their dreams

at all, and most dreams are forgotten by

the time one _____ . Still, some
                    3

dreams seem so _____ , it is
                    4

hard to believe they are only dreams.

several	people
wakes	
continued	real

NUMBER CORRECT × 5 = YOUR SCORE

44

KNOWING HOW TO READ CRITICALLY. Each of the following questions will help you to think critically about the selection. Put an *x* in the box next to the correct answer.

1. Miss Harper's experiences at Ricket's Landing were
   ☐ a. what she expected.
   ☐ b. not too frightening.
   ☐ c. part of a bad dream.

2. Which statement is true?
   ☐ a. The bus driver had trouble waking Miss Harper because she was sleeping so soundly.
   ☐ b. Belle charged Miss Harper $50 for the room.
   ☐ c. When Miss Harper arrived at Ricket's Landing, the sun was shining brightly.

3. We may infer (figure out) that Miss Harper once
   ☐ a. visited Ricket's Landing.
   ☐ b. lived at Belle's roadhouse.
   ☐ c. had a doll named Rosabelle.

4. When she saw the sign "Ricket's Landing" at the end of the story, Miss Harper was probably
   ☐ a. relieved.
   ☐ b. shocked.
   ☐ c. pleased.

Questions for Writing and Discussion
- Do you think Miss Harper was a happy or an unhappy person? Refer to the story to support your answer.
- When Miss Harper opened the closet in the room, what did she discover? Why was she pleased at first? What happened to change her mind?
- At the end of the story, Miss Harper found herself back at Ricket's Landing. What do you suppose will happen now?

Use the boxes below to total your scores for the exercises. Then write your score on pages 150 and 151.

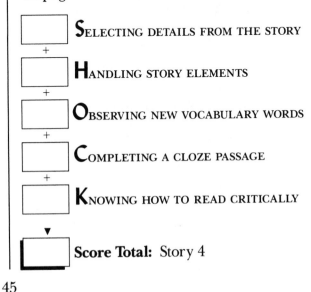

☐ **S**ELECTING DETAILS FROM THE STORY
+
☐ **H**ANDLING STORY ELEMENTS
+
☐ **O**BSERVING NEW VOCABULARY WORDS
+
☐ **C**OMPLETING A CLOZE PASSAGE
+
☐ **K**NOWING HOW TO READ CRITICALLY
▼
☐ **Score Total:** Story 4

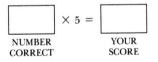

☐ × 5 = ☐

NUMBER   YOUR
CORRECT   SCORE

5

The Tell-Tale Heart

by Edgar Allan Poe

True, nervous—very, very dreadfully nervous, I have been and still am. But why do you say that I am mad? The disease has *sharpened* my senses— not destroyed them—not dulled them. So why then call me mad? Listen to how clearly—how *calmly* I can tell you the whole story.

It is impossible to say when the idea entered my brain. But once it was there, it haunted me day and night. There was no hatred at all. I loved the old man. He had never wronged me. He had never insulted me. For his gold I had no desire. I think it was his eye. Yes, it was his *eye*! One of his eyes was pale blue and dull. It **resembled** the eye of a vulture. Whenever it looked at me, my blood ran cold. And so I finally made up my mind to take the life of the old man—to rid myself of the eye forever.

Now this is the point. You think I am mad. Madmen know nothing. But you should have seen *me*. You should have seen how *wisely*, how cautiously, how skillfully, I went about my work.

I was never kinder to the old man than during the week before I killed him. Every night about midnight I turned the latch to his door and opened it—oh, so gently! I made an opening just large enough for my body to fit through. Then I stepped into the room. I carried a lantern whose light I had turned off. I moved slowly, very, very slowly, so that I might not disturb the old man's sleep. It took me an hour before I reached the old man's bed. Ha!—would a madman have been as wise as this, as clever, as **cunning**? Then I turned on the lantern carefully, oh, so carefully, so carefully that a single thin ray of light fell upon his vulture eye.

This I did for seven long nights—every night just at midnight. But I found the eye always closed. And so it was impossible for me to do my work. For it was not the old man who troubled me, but his evil, his horrible, **hideous** eye.

And every morning at daybreak, I went boldly into his room. I spoke to him courteously and politely. I called him cheerfully by name. I inquired about how well he had slept. So you see, it would have been difficult, very difficult, indeed, for the old man to suspect that every night, just at twelve, I looked upon him while he was sleeping.

On the eighth night, I was even more cautious than usual in opening the door. Never before that night had I felt so powerful—so wise. I could hardly contain my feelings. To think that there I was, opening the door little by little—and he had not the slightest idea of my secret plan or purpose! I almost chuckled at the idea.

Perhaps he heard me, for he moved on the bed suddenly, as if startled. Now you may think that I hesitated or drew back—but no. The room was totally dark, for the shutters were closed. So I knew that he could not see the opening of the door, and I kept pushing it open.

47

I was in the room when my knee suddenly knocked against the lantern. The old man sprang up in bed, crying out, "Who's there?"

I kept quite still and said nothing. For a whole hour I did not move a muscle. But meanwhile I did not hear him lie down. He was sitting up in the bed listening. He was listening—just as I have done, night after night, listening and guarding against—Death.

Soon I heard a low groan. It was not a groan of pain or of grief. Oh, no—it was a groan of *fear.* I knew the sound well. Many a night, just at midnight, when all the world is at sleep, such a groan of terror has escaped from my lips. So, as I say, I knew the sound well.

I knew what the old man felt, and I pitied him—though in my heart I chuckled. I knew that he had been lying awake ever since the first slight noise had awakened him. His fear had been growing since then. He had been trying to convince himself that it was nothing. But he could not. He had been saying to himself, "It was just the wind in the chimney. It was nothing but a mouse scampering across the floor. It was only a cricket which chirped." Yes, he had been trying to comfort himself with these thoughts. But he had been trying in vain. *All in vain.* Because he could sense Death approaching him, although he neither saw nor heard me.

I waited a long time, very patiently, without hearing him lie down. But my mind was made up, and I resolved to act. I turned on the lantern very carefully, so that a single dim ray of light, like the thread of a spider, shone upon his vulture eye.

The eye was open—wide, wide open, and I gazed at it. I saw it plainly and **distinctly.** Its dull blue color chilled me to the bone. I could see no other part of the old man's face or body, for I had directed the ray of light directly on that eye.

Have I not said that what you mistake for madness is the sharpness of my senses? Now I heard a low, dull quick sound—the sound a watch makes when it is wrapped in cotton. I knew *that* sound well, too. It was the beating of the old man's heart. It increased my anger, the way the beating of a drum stirs a soldier to action.

Even so, I held back and kept still. I hardly breathed. I held the lantern as steadily as I could, trying my best to shine its light upon the eye. Meanwhile, the terrible pounding of the heart increased. It grew quicker and quicker and louder and louder every moment. The old man must have been terrified. It grew louder, I say, louder every moment! Do you understand what I am saying? I have told you that I am nervous—and I am. And now, in the dead of night, within the dreadful silence of that old house, the pounding of the heart filled me with a terror I could hardly control.

For several minutes I stood still and did nothing. But the pounding grew even louder. I thought the heart would burst. And now a new fear seized me—that the sound would be heard by a neighbor!

The old man's hour had come! With a loud yell, I rushed across the room. He screamed once—only once. In an instant I dragged him to the floor and pressed the heavy blanket over his face. For many minutes the heart beat on with a muffled sound. This did not trouble me, however. It would not be heard through the walls. Finally it stopped. The old man was dead. I removed the blanket and examined the body. Yes, he was dead, stone dead. I placed my hand on his heart and held it there for many minutes. There was no pulse. He was dead. His eye would trouble me no more.

Do you still think me mad? You will think so no longer when you hear the wise steps I took to hide the body.

The night was growing late, and I worked hastily but in silence. I removed several wide boards from the floor of the room. Into the empty space I carefully placed the body. I then nailed back the boards so carefully, so skillfully, that no human eye—not even *his*— could notice they had been touched.

It was four o'clock when I finished my work. As the bell sounded the hour, there was a knocking at the street door. I went down to open it with a light heart—for what had I *now* to fear?

Three police officers politely introduced themselves. A scream had been heard by the neighbors during the night. Foul play was suspected. They had been sent to search the house.

I smiled—for *what* had I to fear? I welcomed the officers warmly. The scream, I said, was my own, in a dream. The old man, I explained, had gone to the country. I took my visitors all through the house. I bid them search, search *well.*

I led them, finally, to *his* room. I showed them his treasures, safe and secure. So filled with confidence was I that I brought chairs into the room and invited the officers to rest *here* from their labors. In the wild joy of my perfect triumph, I placed my own chair *right on top of the very spot* beneath which lay buried the corpse of my victim!

The officers were satisfied. My calm manner convinced them I had nothing to hide. But before long I felt myself getting pale. I wished they would leave. My head ached, and I thought that I heard a ringing in my ears. But still they sat and kept chatting.

The ringing became clearer—it continued and became louder. I talked more and more to get rid of the ringing. But still it grew louder. And finally I realized that the noise was coming from somewhere *outside* of my ears!

I know that I grew very pale. I began talking faster and still louder. Yet the sound increased—and what could I do! It was *a low, dull quick sound— the sound a watch makes when it is wrapped in cotton.*

I gasped for breath—but the officers did not hear me. I talked more rapidly and even louder, but the noise kept increasing. I got up from my chair. I shouted. I swung my arms around wildly. But the noise still grew louder. *Why wouldn't the officers go?*

I paced back and forth wildly. And still the sound grew louder! What could I do? I yelled! I screamed! I grabbed the chair upon which I had been sitting and banged it against the floor. But the noise drowned out everything and grew louder. It grew louder—louder—*louder!* And still the officers chatted pleasantly—and smiled.

Was it possible they did not hear? No, no! They heard! They suspected! They knew! They were making fun of my terror! They were mocking my agony!

I could no longer stand their horrible, knowing smiles. I felt that I must scream or die. And now—again—listen. Listen! I hear it louder! Louder! *Louder!*

"Stop it!" I screamed at the officers. "Smile at me no more! I admit the deed! Tear up the boards. Here! Over here! What you hear is the beating of his terrible heart!"

SELECTING DETAILS FROM THE STORY.
Each of the following sentences helps you understand the story. Complete each sentence below by putting an *x* in the box next to the correct answer.

1. The narrator (person who tells the story) decided to kill the old man
   □ a. to get the old man's gold.
   □ b. because the old man had insulted him.
   □ c. to rid himself of the old man's eye.

2. During the course of the story, the narrator thought that he heard
   □ a. the beating of the old man's heart.
   □ b. screams coming from the old man's room.
   □ c. the neighbors laughing at him.

3. The narrator hid the old man's body in
   □ a. a closet.
   □ b. a space under the floor.
   □ c. the basement.

4. At the end of the story, the narrator told the police
   □ a. to forgive him.
   □ b. to get out.
   □ c. where to find the body.

HANDLING STORY ELEMENTS. Each of the following questions reviews your understanding of story elements. Put an *x* in the box next to the correct answer to each question.

1. What happened first in the *plot* of "The Tell-Tale Heart"?
   □ a. The narrator slipped into the room and turned on the lantern.
   □ b. The narrator grabbed his chair and banged it against the floor.
   □ c. Three police officers appeared at the door.

2. Which word best *characterizes* the narrator?
   □ a. generous
   □ b. helpful
   □ c. mad

3. Because of the author's *style* of writing, "The Tell-Tale Heart" may be *characterized* as a
   □ a. mystery story.
   □ b. love story.
   □ c. tale of horror.

4. Which sentence best tells the *theme* of the story?
   □ a. A murderer, haunted by his deed, finally confesses to the crime.
   □ b. When an old man hears a noise in his room at night, he sits up in bed listening.
   □ c. Police officers search a house because screams have been heard.

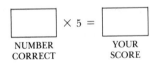

NUMBER CORRECT   × 5 =   YOUR SCORE

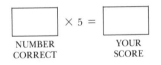

NUMBER CORRECT   × 5 =   YOUR SCORE

OBSERVING NEW VOCABULARY WORDS. Answer the following vocabulary questions by putting an *x* in the box next to the correct answer. The vocabulary words are printed in **boldface** in the story. If you wish, look back at the words before you answer the questions.

1. One of his eyes was pale blue and dull; it resembled the eye of a vulture. The word *resembled* means
   ☐ a. looked like.
   ☐ b. searched for.
   ☐ c. attacked.

2. He gazed at the eye and saw it plainly and distinctly. What is the meaning of the word *distinctly*?
   ☐ a. dimly
   ☐ b. clearly
   ☐ c. foolishly

3. "Would a madman have been as wise as this, as clever, as cunning?" As used here, the word *cunning* means
   ☐ a. sly.
   ☐ b. helpless.
   ☐ c. ridiculous.

4. "It was not the old man who troubled me, but his horrible, hideous eye." What is the meaning of the word *hideous*?
   ☐ a. unusual or rare
   ☐ b. handsome or attractive
   ☐ c. very ugly or frightful

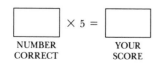

NUMBER CORRECT   × 5 =   YOUR SCORE

COMPLETING A CLOZE PASSAGE. Complete the following paragraph by filling in each blank with one of the words listed in the box below. Each of the words appears in the story. Since there are five words and four blanks, one word in the group will not be used.

The heart is a _____ organ
               1

that pumps blood to all parts of the

body. Located in the center of the

chest, the heart is protected by a tough

_____. The heart weighs a
    2

little _____ than half a pound
         3

and is only about the size of a fist.

But during the course of a day, it

_____ more than 100,000 times.
    4

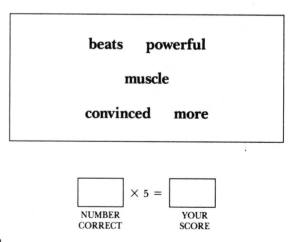

beats   powerful

muscle

convinced   more

NUMBER CORRECT   × 5 =   YOUR SCORE

KNOWING HOW TO READ CRITICALLY. Each of the following questions will help you to think critically about the selection. Put an *x* in the box next to the correct answer.

1. The first paragraph of the story indicates that the narrator was
   - ☐ a. in perfect health.
   - ☐ b. suffering from some kind of disease.
   - ☐ c. upset about what he had done.

2. Which statement is true?
   - ☐ a. The narrator tried to prove that he was not mad by explaining how skillfully he arranged the murder.
   - ☐ b. The police accused the narrator of murdering the old man.
   - ☐ c. For weeks the old man had known that someone was trying to murder him.

3. The narrator was convinced that the police
   - ☐ a. knew where the old man was buried.
   - ☐ b. had seen him commit the crime.
   - ☐ c. could hear the beating of the old man's heart.

4. At the end of the story, the narrator
   - ☐ a. ran wildly out of the house.
   - ☐ b. fought with the police.
   - ☐ c. confessed.

Questions for Writing and Discussion

- The narrator said, "Listen to how clearly—how *calmly* I can tell you the whole story." To whom is the narrator telling the story? Under what conditions? Explain your answers.
- The narrator thought that the police were making fun of him. Why did he think that? Give several reasons.
- "A guilty conscience needs no accuser." What is the meaning of that saying? Explain how it applies to the story.

Use the boxes below to total your scores for the exercises. Then write your score on pages 150 and 151.

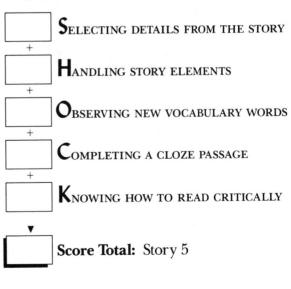

☐ **S**ELECTING DETAILS FROM THE STORY
+
☐ **H**ANDLING STORY ELEMENTS
+
☐ **O**BSERVING NEW VOCABULARY WORDS
+
☐ **C**OMPLETING A CLOZE PASSAGE
+
☐ **K**NOWING HOW TO READ CRITICALLY
▼
☐ **Score Total:** Story 5

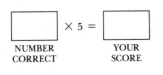

☐ × 5 = ☐

NUMBER   YOUR
CORRECT   SCORE

6

Otero's Visitor

by Manuela Williams Crosno

Many years ago there came to this land from Spain a noble family named Otero. Many sons there were who owned much gold, so the family was able to establish itself well in their new country.

One of the sons, Adolfo, built a beautiful hacienda[1] for himself. He furnished it with the possessions the family had brought with them from Spain. The most magnificent of these was an organ, which stood in one corner of the long living room near the fireplace. It was beautifully made of carved wood and was supported by heavy carved legs. The organ had been brought from Spain to Mexico City. From there it had been transported northward, a journey of three months, by oxcart.

Many sons and daughters were born in the hacienda of Adolfo Otero. It became a place of laughter and song and music. Happy indeed were those who dwelled within its walls.

As Adolfo grew older, his children married and established haciendas for themselves. Now Adolfo lived alone except for his wife and two servants. But still there came to his house many who were friends. And from time to time weary travelers arrived. They had heard of Adolfo's hospitality and were glad to stop there for a night on their journey.

This is a country of many winds. Sometimes the soft winds blow from

---

1. **hacienda:** Spanish for "a large estate, ranch, or country house."

the southwest and travel close to the ground. They are the winds that sing songs in the yucca[2] and in the grasses that grow on the mesa. But sometimes the hard winds blow from the east. They bring snow, if it is winter, or sand. The sand blows hard into the face of the traveler and his horse so that he is forced to seek shelter.

One day there came such a wind. All day long it beat against the hacienda of Adolfo Otero. It blew the white sands and the brown sands in drifts against the doors and windows. No one ventured out on this day. Even when the sun vanished behind the mountains, the wind did not **diminish**. In the darkness of the night, it blew even harder. It seemed worse than it had been in the daytime.

The two servants and Otero's wife retired early. But Adolfo remained in the living room. He paced back and forth, back and forth, with a very confident step. It was as if he were telling the wind and the sand that he was calm and at peace.

Then Adolfo seated himself in front of the fireplace where he sat looking at the **embers**, dreaming who-knows-what dreams. A handsome figure he made sitting there, his white hair falling down to his shoulders. His black eyes glowed like coals as the light before him flickered and threw shadows upon the wall. He wore a black jacket, trimmed in fine black satin, and black trousers. Around his waist a brightly colored sash was tied.

Suddenly his dreams were interrupted by a loud pounding on the door. Adolfo pulled up the heavy bar that served as a lock. The great carved door swung open to admit a stranger. He seemed greatly upset. He refused to remove his hat or to warm himself in front of the fire. He was a young man, powerfully built. His thick black beard stood out sharply from the pale face beneath it.

"They are coming!" he said, as though Adolfo knew who "they" might be. "*This* they must not find!" And he drew from his coat a small carved wooden box. This he thrust into Adolfo's hand.

"You shall hide this for me, and when I return you shall give it to me. Guard it with your life! Hide it carefully and tell no one!" With these words

---

2. **yucca:** a plant found in the southwestern part of the United States.

the man turned, opened the door, and then closed it quickly behind him. A moment later, Adolfo heard the sound of hoofs as the stranger rode quickly away.

Amazed, Adolfo stood and held the little carved box. Then he walked closer to the fireplace and examined it. It was curiously carved, but whether or not it was locked, Adolfo never knew. For he was a Spanish gentleman—a caballero—and he never considered opening it.

Then remembering the command of his visitor, Adolfo walked over to the old organ. He opened a secret panel in one of the heavy wooden legs. He carefully **inserted** the box in the space. Then he closed the panel. Adolfo smiled to himself with satisfaction because he had been able to hide the box so well. Even his wife did not know of this secret place.

He went back and sat down in front of the fire. Soon there was a clatter of hoofs, and three armed men stood in his doorway.

"Has anyone stopped here?" they asked, glancing around the room. "Have you heard anyone pass by?"

Adolfo held his head to one side as if thinking. "A few minutes ago," he said, "I heard a horse's hoofs flying down the road in a great hurry."

The men left at once to give chase.

As the years passed by, Adolfo did not forget the stranger who had placed a box in his keeping. He waited for the return of the man and never thought to open the secret panel until then. And one day Adolfo died, taking with him the secret of the little carved box and its hiding place.

The eldest son, Reyes, moved into the hacienda with his wife, Carla. He wished to be near his mother, who was by now quite old.

Occasionally Reyes would plan a fiesta to honor the old days. Then the hacienda would ring with the laughter of young people and old. The good people would sit by the fireplace. They would speak of Adolfo and of the many fine times they had enjoyed under his roof. The younger ones would gather around the organ and sing songs.

"This is a fine instrument," says Reyes. "Each day its tone becomes more and more mellow."

One moonlit night when the wind was howling, Carla was awakened by a sound in the house. She arose quickly and walked to the living room door. She stopped just outside the room and listened. Yes, she was sure of what she heard! There were footsteps walking slowly in the room—back and forth, back and forth! Quiet, confident footsteps!

Carla opened the door, but could see no one in the moonlit room. She walked across to the organ and back, but no one was there.

In the morning Carla told her husband, and that night he too listened. But they heard nothing. For six nights they listened without hearing anything. On the seventh night, the wind was howling loudly. Then they heard the footsteps walking confidently—back and forth, back and forth, the full length of the living room. But when Reyes and Carla entered the room, no one was there!

Soon they learned to expect the footsteps just before ten o'clock on nights when the wind howled. And promptly, at ten-thirty, the footsteps would cease and not be heard again. Reyes and Carla might have been frightened. But there was something familiar about the steps which calmed and **reassured** them.

They said nothing of this to the wife of Adolfo, for they feared it would alarm her. Great was the surprise of Reyes, therefore, to discover his mother walking back and forth in the living room one morning. For a moment Reyes thought it might have been she whom he and his wife had heard. But no—his mother's footsteps were much lighter. Besides, she could hardly have disappeared so quickly.

So Reyes asked, "Mamacita, what are you doing here?"

She looked at him for a moment, quietly, then answered. "Your father has been walking in this room many nights. I am trying to find what is disturbing his spirit."

Reyes knew then that the footsteps he heard were the footsteps of his father. Many times he had heard him walking just that way. That was why, he thought, they did not frighten or alarm him. He knew them so well.

Reyes said to his mother, "Do not be distressed. Father was a good man. We will learn what is disturbing him. I will help you." And he patted her gently on her stooped shoulders.

Each evening when the wind howled, Reyes remained alone in the

living room. He sat quietly in front of the fireplace, looking almost like his father. But although he heard the footsteps, nothing further happened.

Then one Friday there came a violent sandstorm. All day the wind whirled the sand in heaps against the hacienda. No one ventured to leave the house. After the sun had set, the wind seemed to increase in fury. But Reyes sat before the fireplace waiting, waiting for—he knew not what.

Suddenly there came a loud knocking at the door. Reyes opened it to admit a stranger. The man looked at him uncertainly in the dim light. Reyes closed the door and pushed the heavy bar against it to keep out the wind and the sand. The stranger seemed quite upset. He was a middle-aged man, powerfully built, with a thick black beard.

Without sitting down the stranger began, "I . . . I thought you were Otero—Señor Adolfo Otero! As I passed by the window I saw you sitting there, and I thought—"

Reyes added, "He was my father."

The man hesitated. He seemed to be making up his mind whether or not to inform Reyes of the purpose of his visit. Then he spoke. "A son of Adolfo Otero could not be other than trustworthy. I have come for a box I left in your father's care."

"Come," said Reyes, "sit here."

And he pointed the stranger to a chair in front of the fireplace. The man sat down without removing his coat.

"Make yourself comfortable," said Reyes. "You are chilled from the wind. I do not know where my father left your box, but I will try to think of where it might be. Let me bring you something warm to drink."

The stranger did not answer. He sat in the chair, looking silently at the fire.

Just as Reyes reached the door, he heard the footsteps. The man by the fireplace heard them, too. Reyes could tell this by the startled look in the stranger's eyes. The man quickly rose to his feet and stared at Reyes.

Reyes smiled. "Do not be alarmed," he said calmly.

The footsteps had walked over to the organ and had stopped. Reyes closed the door behind him. A few moments later he returned.

The outside door stood open. The stranger had disappeared. Reyes stood in the room and looked around him. As he did, he saw a small panel in the leg of the organ sliding softly shut. Then he heard the footsteps for the last time. The wind from the entrance blew the door to the patio open, and the curtains parted as if someone had gently walked through them.

Reyes closed the outer door against the fury of the wind. He hurried to the organ and stooped to examine the place he had seen slide shut. His fingers found the secret panel and pushed it open. The little hiding place was empty!

SELECTING DETAILS FROM THE STORY.
Each of the following sentences helps
you understand the story. Complete each
sentence below by putting an *x* in the
box next to the correct answer.

1. The stranger ordered Otero to
   □ a. give him a horse.
   □ b. guard a small wooden box.
   □ c. protect him from some enemies.

2. Otero hid the little carved box
   □ a. by burying it in the yard.
   □ b. between some bricks in the
      fireplace.
   □ c. in a panel in the organ.

3. One night when the wind was howling,
   Carla was awakened by
   □ a. the sound of footsteps.
   □ b. loud shouting.
   □ c. rifle shots.

4. At the end of the story, Reyes
   discovered that the
   □ a. organ had been damaged.
   □ b. secret hiding place was empty.
   □ c. stranger had left a gold coin.

HANDLING STORY ELEMENTS. Each of
the following questions reviews your
understanding of story elements. Put
an *x* in the box next to the correct
answer to each question.

1. What happened last in the *plot* of
   "Otero's Visitor"?
   □ a. Three armed men came to
      Adolfo's door.
   □ b. Reyes saw a panel in the leg of
      the organ slide shut.
   □ c. A stranger thrust a small wooden
      box into Adolfo's hand.

2. Which sentence best *characterizes* the
   stranger?
   □ a. He was powerfully built, with
      a thick black beard.
   □ b. He had long white hair and wore
      a black satin jacket.
   □ c. He seemed tired and weak.

3. "A son of Adolfo Otero could not be
   other than trustworthy." That line of
   dialogue was spoken by
   □ a. Reyes.
   □ b. Carla.
   □ c. the stranger.

4. Which of the following best describes
   the *mood* of the story?
   □ a. humorous
   □ b. serious
   □ c. terrifying

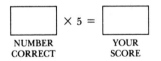

NUMBER CORRECT   × 5 =   YOUR SCORE

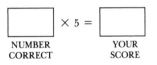

NUMBER CORRECT   × 5 =   YOUR SCORE

OBSERVING NEW VOCABULARY WORDS. Answer the following vocabulary questions by putting an *x* in the box next to the correct answer. The vocabulary words are printed in **boldface** in the story. If you wish, look back at the words before you answer the questions.

1. He opened a secret panel and carefully inserted the box in the space. The word *inserted* means
   ☐ a. lost.
   ☐ b. put in.
   ☐ c. imagined.

2. Adolfo seated himself in front of the fireplace where he sat looking at the embers. What are *embers*?
   ☐ a. paintings
   ☐ b. photographs
   ☐ c. glowing ashes

3. Something familiar about the sound of the steps reassured Carla and Reyes. Which of the following best defines the word *reassured*?
   ☐ a. startled
   ☐ b. leaped at
   ☐ c. gave confidence to

4. When the sun went down, the wind did not diminish; it blew even harder in the darkness. What is the meaning of the word *diminish*?
   ☐ a. decrease
   ☐ b. stun
   ☐ c. howl

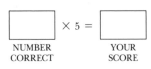

NUMBER CORRECT   × 5 =   YOUR SCORE

COMPLETING A CLOZE PASSAGE. Complete the following paragraph by filling in each blank with one of the words listed in the box below. Each of the words appears in the story. Since there are five words and four blanks, one word in the group will not be used.

The Museum of International Folk

Art in Santa Fe, New _____,
                                    1

contains the largest collection of folk art

in the world. Included are toys, dolls,

costumes, and masks from more than

100 _____. One wing alone
                2

houses thousands of examples of

_____ folk art. The museum
        3

offers tours to help visitors _____
                                        4

their experience even more.

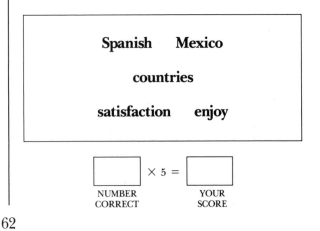

Spanish   Mexico

countries

satisfaction   enjoy

NUMBER CORRECT   × 5 =   YOUR SCORE

KNOWING HOW TO READ CRITICALLY. Each of the following questions will help you to think critically about the selection. Put an *x* in the box next to the correct answer.

1. Clues in the story suggest that Adolfo couldn't rest easily until
   ☐ a. the box he accepted was returned to its owner.
   ☐ b. he felt certain that his children were happy.
   ☐ c. he was sure that his wife was well taken care of.

2. We may infer that the stranger obtained the wooden box from
   ☐ a. Reyes.
   ☐ b. Carla.
   ☐ c. the spirit of Adolfo.

3. Which statement is true?
   ☐ a. Adolfo told his wife where the box was hidden.
   ☐ b. When the stranger heard the footsteps, he became alarmed.
   ☐ c. The stranger decided not to tell Reyes the purpose of his visit.

4. After the stranger left, the spirit of Adolfo
   ☐ a. ran after him.
   ☐ b. sat down in the living room.
   ☐ c. disappeared, never to return.

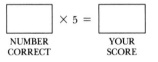

NUMBER
CORRECT   × 5 =   YOUR
                      SCORE

Questions for Writing and Discussion

- "Otero's Visitor" may be described as a ghost story. Do you agree or disagree with that statement? Explain your answer.
- The wind plays an important part in "Otero's Visitor." Find examples from the story to support that statement.
- What do you suppose was in the little box that the stranger left with Adolfo? Why do you think the men were chasing the stranger? Make up a brief story as you answer those questions.

Use the boxes below to total your scores for the exercises. Then write your score on pages 150 and 151.

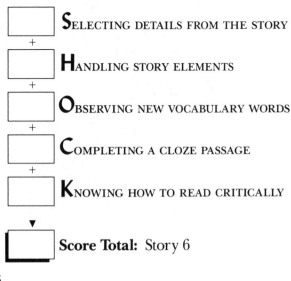

☐ SELECTING DETAILS FROM THE STORY
+
☐ HANDLING STORY ELEMENTS
+
☐ OBSERVING NEW VOCABULARY WORDS
+
☐ COMPLETING A CLOZE PASSAGE
+
☐ KNOWING HOW TO READ CRITICALLY
▼
☐ **Score Total:** Story 6

7

The Falcon

by Giovanni Boccaccio

The tale is told of a young man named Federigo who lived in the city of Florence in Italy many years ago. This Federigo was famous for his courage and his gallant deeds. As chance would have it, he fell in love with Mona Giovanna, one of the most beautiful and charming women in the city.

Federigo sent her splendid and expensive gifts. He held feasts and banquets in her honor. But Mona Giovanna did not care for Federigo's gifts. She married another man—and to him she was as true as she was fair.

Since Federigo continued to spend his money recklessly, his riches soon **dwindled** away. Before long, all he owned were just two things of value. One was a little farm from which he gained a modest income. The other was a falcon which had no equal anywhere.

Seeing that he could no longer afford to live in the city, Federigo moved to Campi to stay on his farm. There, without owing anything to anyone, he flew his falcon whenever he could and put up with his poverty without complaining.

Meanwhile, Mona Giovanna's husband was badly injured in a hunting accident. Realizing that death was near, he drew up his will. He named his wife and their son as his heirs, and soon afterward he died.

Mona Giovanna was now a widow. That summer, according to the custom, she went away to the country with her son, there to **mourn** the loss of her husband. As it happened, she stayed in a cottage near Federigo's farm. The boy soon became friendly with Federigo, and they spent many happy hours together hunting and flying the falcon. In fact, the boy took such delight in the falcon that he wanted it for his own. But he did not dare ask for it, seeing how dear it was to Federigo.

Much to his mother's grief, the boy fell ill about this time. Mona Giovanna, who had no other children, loved and **cherished** him dearly. All day long she was at his bedside, comforting him, and asking him over and over if there was anything he wanted, and promising him that if it could be obtained, she would surely get it for him.

After hearing her say this so often, the boy finally replied, "Mother, if you could get Federigo's falcon for me, I'm sure I would get well."

When the lady heard this, she was at first taken aback. She hesitated at this request and wondered what to do. She was aware that Federigo had long been in love with her, and that she had never so much as given him a glance. She thought, "How can I possibly go or send to Federigo and ask him for his falcon, which is, I hear, the finest one that ever flew? How can I be so selfish as to want to take it away from him when he takes such delight in it?"

Troubled by these thoughts, and knowing that she had only to ask for the falcon to receive it, she did not know what to say. She did not answer her son at first, but remained silent. Finally, she allowed her love of the boy to get the better of her pride, and she determined to make him content at any cost. She decided not to send for the falcon but to fetch it herself.

"My son," she said, "be of good cheer and do your best to get well and strong again. I promise that tomorrow morning I'll go myself for the falcon and bring it back to you."

The boy smiled, and showed a strong improvement that very day.

The following morning, Mona Giovanna, accompanied by another woman, went to Federigo's house and asked for him. As it was, he happened to be in his garden taking care of some chores. When he heard that Mona Giovanna was at the door asking for him, he was greatly surprised and he hurried to greet her.

Upon seeing her, he bowed deeply. Mona Giovanna said, "Good day to you, Federigo. I hope that you are well. I am sorry for all the harm you have suffered through me by placing more love in me than you should have. I should like to show friendship by having lunch with you and this friend of mine."

Humbly, Federigo replied, "I don't remember ever having suffered any harm through you. Indeed, though you have come to a poor host, your visit is more dear to me than it would have been had I still had my fortune."

With these words, he **escorted** Mona Giovanna and her friend into his house and from there into the garden. He said, with embarrassment, "Since I have no one to help me prepare lunch, would you be kind enough to rest here with your friend while I make the meal and see that the table is set."

Federigo, of course, was very poor. But not until that moment, despite his terrible poverty, had he really been so aware of the state to which he had been reduced by wasting his wealth. When he realized that he had nothing special to serve the lady he loved, he suddenly was shocked. He rushed wildly up and down the house, searching here and there, everywhere, for something to serve, or something of value to sell for food. But nothing did he find.

By now the hour was growing late, and Federigo was more anxious than ever. Back and forth he paced, bitterly grieving, and almost out of his senses. But finally he found something which he felt was appropriate, and he began to make lunch.

The table was set with the best linen he still had. Then joining Mona Giovanna in the garden, his face beaming with happiness, Federigo said, "What modest dinner I can furnish is now ready." The lady rose with her friend, and they took their places at the table. There Federigo served them with the greatest care and devotion.

When the dinner was over, they spent some time in pleasant conversation. Then Mona Giovanna, thinking that the time had come to bring up the subject of her visit, addressed him cautiously.

"I am sure, Federigo," she said, "that you'll be amazed at my boldness when I confess the main reason for my visit, and when you hear what I am going to ask of you. But if you had children of your own, you would know how great is the love one bears them. And then you would understand and, perhaps, even forgive me.

"But though you have none, I, who have one, must, despite myself— and though it pains me to do it—ask something of you. I know it is the dearest thing you have. It is your falcon, Federigo. It is your falcon which my little boy wants so much that if I don't bring it to him, I greatly fear that his illness may take a turn for the worse, and I might even lose him. I beg you then, Federigo, not for the love you bear me, for you owe it nothing, but for your own noble spirit and kindness—which you have proved so many times by your worthy deeds. I beg you to give me your falcon. In that way I may save my son's life by your gift, and he will be in debt to you for as long as he lives."

When Federigo heard what Mona Giovanna was asking, tears welled up in his eyes before he could say a word. Mona Giovanna believed that his grief was caused by the thought of parting with his falcon, and she was about to tell him that she did not want it. But she held back and waited to hear what he had to say.

"Dear lady," he said, drying his tears, "since the day I first fell in love with you, I've had many an occasion to complain of my fate. But all of my misfortunes were nothing compared to what fate makes me suffer right now. I must never be at peace again thinking about how you came to see me in my poor little cottage where you never set foot when I was rich. And you asked me for a little gift, and must hear me say that it is impossible for me to grant it to you. Listen and I shall tell you why it cannot be.

"When I heard that you wished to dine with me, I thought it only right to serve you the most excellent meal I could possibly afford. Therefore, thinking of the falcon which you now ask of me, I judged it worthy of you. And today you had it served roasted on a platter."

And to prove his words, he showed her the bird's feathers and beak.

At first the lady blamed him for sacrificing so much for her. But, at the same time, she could not help but admire his generous spirit. Realizing, however, that she had no hope of obtaining the falcon, and greatly concerned about her child's recovery, she thanked Federigo for the honor he had paid her, and returned to the bedside of her son. Whether the boy was disappointed because he could not have the falcon or whether he was too ill to ever recover, he soon breathed his last, to his mother's great sorrow.

For a long time Mona Giovanna remained tearful and grieving. The seasons passed slowly, and after a time she began to feel better. Her brothers urged her to marry again.

Then one day, she began to think of Federigo. She thought of his kindness and his warm smile and of how he had sacrificed his marvelous falcon for her. Finally she said to her brothers, "I'd be glad to marry again. But the only person I'll marry will be Federigo."

This surprised them and they said, "How foolish! How can you marry a man who hasn't any money to his name?"

She answered, "I know very well what you say is true. But I'd rather have a man in need of wealth, than wealth in need of a man."

And so it came to pass that Federigo finally saw himself married to the woman he had loved for so long. And they lived together in happiness to the end of their days.

SELECTING DETAILS FROM THE STORY.
Each of the following sentences helps
you understand the story. Complete each
sentence below by putting an x in the
box next to the correct answer.

1. After Federigo fell in love with
   Mona Giovanna, he sent her
   ☐ a. many expensive gifts.
   ☐ b. several love letters.
   ☐ c. an invitation to dinner.

2. Mona Giovanna went to Federigo's
   farm in order to ask him for
   ☐ a. money.
   ☐ b. advice about her son.
   ☐ c. his falcon.

3. Federigo rushed wildly up and down
   the house searching for
   ☐ a. a tablecloth.
   ☐ b. something to serve.
   ☐ c. some flowers.

4. At the end of the story, Mona Giovanna
   and Federigo
   ☐ a. decided never to see each other
      again.
   ☐ b. fought over the falcon.
   ☐ c. got married.

HANDLING STORY ELEMENTS. Each of
the following questions reviews your
understanding of story elements. Put
an x in the box next to the correct
answer to each question.

1. "The Falcon" is *set*
   ☐ a. on a farm in France.
   ☐ b. somewhere in California.
   ☐ c. in Italy many years ago.

2. What happened first in the *plot* of
   the story?
   ☐ a. Mona Giovanna and a friend ate
      lunch with Federigo.
   ☐ b. Federigo held feasts and banquets
      in Mona Giovanna's honor.
   ☐ c. The son of Mona Giovanna died.

3. Which group of words best *characterizes*
   Mona Giovanna?
   ☐ a. beautiful; charming; devoted
   ☐ b. foolish; proud; calm
   ☐ c. thoughtless; moody; poor

4. Which sentence best tells the *theme* of
   "The Falcon"?
   ☐ a. When a man makes a sacrifice
      for the woman he loves, it
      eventually leads to their marriage.
   ☐ b. A man and a boy spend many
      happy hours together, hunting
      and·flying a falcon.
   ☐ c. A woman's brothers urge her to
      get married.

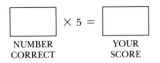

☐ × 5 = ☐

NUMBER   YOUR
CORRECT   SCORE

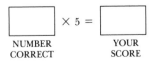

☐ × 5 = ☐

NUMBER   YOUR
CORRECT   SCORE

OBSERVING NEW VOCABULARY WORDS. Answer the following vocabulary questions by putting an *x* in the box next to the correct answer. The vocabulary words are printed in **boldface** in the story. If you wish, look back at the words before you answer the questions.

1. After her husband died, Mona Giovanna went to the country to mourn her loss. Which of the following best defines the word *mourn*?
   ☐ a. feel or show grief for
   ☐ b. speak in a loud voice
   ☐ c. challenge or threaten

2. Mona Giovanna loved and cherished her only child. The word *cherished* means
   ☐ a. neglected.
   ☐ b. bothered or troubled.
   ☐ c. cared about tenderly.

3. Federigo escorted Mona Giovanna into his house and then into the garden. What is the meaning of the word *escorted*?
   ☐ a. accompanied
   ☐ b. stumbled
   ☐ c. doubted

4. Because he spent his money wildly, Federigo's riches soon dwindled away. The word *dwindled* means
   ☐ a. increased.
   ☐ b. shrank.
   ☐ c. earned.

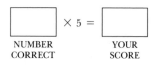

NUMBER
CORRECT × 5 = YOUR
SCORE

COMPLETING A CLOZE PASSAGE. Complete the following paragraph by filling in each blank with one of the words listed in the box below. Each of the words appears in the story. Since there are five words and four blanks, one word in the group will not be used.

The peregrine falcon is one of the fiercest _____ in the world.

It _____ small animals by swooping down on them from heights of several hundred feet. During these tremendous dives, the falcon can reach a speed of 150 miles per _____ or more. The falcon's feet strike the animal with _____ force, killing it or knocking it out.

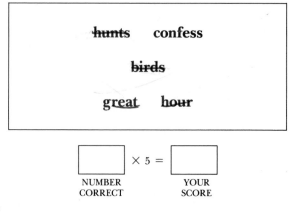

~~hunts~~   confess

~~birds~~

~~great~~   ~~hour~~

NUMBER
CORRECT × 5 = YOUR
SCORE

72

KNOWING HOW TO READ CRITICALLY. Each of the following questions will help you to think critically about the selection. Put an *x* in the box next to the correct answer.

1. Federigo did not give Mona Giovanna the falcon because he
   - ☐ a. was angry with her.
   - ☐ b. loved it too much to give up.
   - ☐ c. had served it for lunch.

2. After Federigo heard Mona Giovanna's request, he
   - ☐ a. shook his head angrily.
   - ☐ b. wiped tears from his eyes.
   - ☐ c. laughed sadly.

3. Federigo showed Mona Giovanna the falcon's feathers and beak because he wanted to
   - ☐ a. shock her.
   - ☐ b. make her feel sorry for him.
   - ☐ c. demonstrate that he was telling the truth.

4. When Mona Giovanna told Federigo that she would marry him, he probably felt
   - ☐ a. surprised and pleased.
   - ☐ b. annoyed.
   - ☐ c. suspicious.

Questions for Writing and Discussion

- Although Mona Giovanna wanted the falcon for her son, she hesitated to ask Federigo for it. Why? Give as many reasons as you can. Why did Mona Giovanna change her mind?
- Mona Giovanna said that she would rather have "a man in need of wealth, than wealth in need of a man." What did she mean by that statement? Do you think she was right? Explain.
- Suppose that Mona Giovanna's son had been given the falcon. Do you think he would have lived? Explain your answer.

Use the boxes below to total your scores for the exercises. Then write your score on pages 150 and 151.

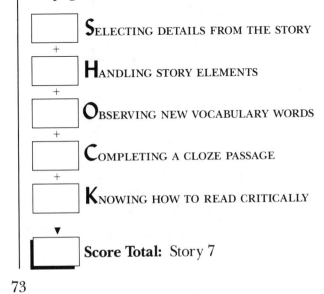

☐   **S**ELECTING DETAILS FROM THE STORY
   +
☐   **H**ANDLING STORY ELEMENTS
   +
☐   **O**BSERVING NEW VOCABULARY WORDS
   +
☐   **C**OMPLETING A CLOZE PASSAGE
   +
☐   **K**NOWING HOW TO READ CRITICALLY
   ▼
☐   **Score Total:** Story 7

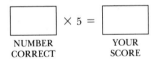

☐ × 5 = ☐

NUMBER   YOUR
CORRECT   SCORE

8

The Leopard Man's Story

by Jack London

*H*e had a dreamy, faraway look in his eyes, and his voice was sad and gentle. He was the Leopard Man, though he did not look it. He earned a good living by appearing in a cage with leopards in front of large audiences. And the more daring he was—the more dangerous his feats—the more he was paid.

As I say, he did not look particularly threatening or powerful. He was slender and pale with narrow, sloping shoulders. He was not actually gloomy, but one sensed that he carried with him a gentle sadness.

My newspaper had sent me to interview him, and for an hour I had been trying to get a story out of him. I wanted something about the terrible **perils** of his work. But to him there was nothing especially thrilling about what he did, nothing very exciting.

Lions? Oh, yes, he said, he had fought with them. It was nothing. All you had to do was pay attention. Anybody could whip a lion with an ordinary stick. He had fought one for half an hour once. Just hit him on the nose every time he rushed. And when the beast changed his **tactics** and charged with his head down, why the thing to do was to stick out your leg. When the lion grabbed at the leg, you just drew it back and hit him on the nose again. That was all. All in a day's work, he said. He made it sound easy.

With a faraway look in his eyes, he showed me his scars. There were many of them. He showed me a recent one where a tiger had slapped at his shoulder and slashed him to the bone. His right arm, from the elbow down, looked as though it had gone through a threshing machine. His injuries had been caused by claws and by fangs. "But it is really nothing," he said. "Only the old wounds bother me once in a while when the rainy weather comes."

Suddenly his face brightened as he remembered something, for he was really as anxious to give me a good story as I was to get it.

"I suppose you've heard of the lion tamer who was hated by another man?" he asked.

He paused and looked thoughtfully at a sick lion in a cage near us.

"This poor lion here has a toothache," he explained. He turned back to me. "Well, as I was saying, the lion tamer used to put his head in a lion's mouth. That was the highlight of his act. The man who hated the lion tamer attended every performance in the hope that one day the lion would crunch down. He followed the show all over the country. The years went by and the man grew old, and the lion tamer grew old, and the lion grew old. And at last one day, he saw what he had waited for. The lion crunched down. And believe me, there wasn't any need to call a doctor."

The Leopard Man glanced casually over his fingernails and shook his head sadly.

"Now that's what I call patience," he continued. "And it's my style. But it was not the style of a fellow I knew. He was a circus performer—a sword-swallower and juggler named DeVille. His wife worked at the circus, too. She did trapeze work. She used to dive from near the roof, into a net, turning over once on the way down, as graceful as you please.

"This DeVille had a quick temper, as quick as his hand, and his hand was as quick as the paw of a tiger. One day, the ringmaster insulted DeVille's wife. When DeVille heard about it, he shoved him against the wooden backboard that he used in his knife-throwing act. He did it so fast, the ringmaster didn't have time to think. And there, right before the audience, DeVille kept the air on fire with his knives, sinking them into the wood all around the ringmaster, so close some of them just touched his clothes.

"The clowns had to pull the knives out to get him loose because he was pinned tight. So the word got around to be careful of DeVille. And no one ever had a harsh word to say about his wife again.

"But there was one man, Wallace, who was afraid of nothing. This Wallace was the lion tamer, and he had the very same trick of putting his head into the lion's mouth. He'd put his head into the mouth of any circus lion, though he preferred Old Augustus, a big, good-natured beast who could always be depended upon.

"As I was saying, Wallace—
'King' Wallace we called him—was
afraid of nothing. He was a king, make
no mistake about it. I've seen him go into
the cage of a lion that had turned wild and,
without a stick, tame him by hitting him on
the nose using just his bare fist.

"One day, King Wallace, in a playful mood, made fun of the juggling
act that DeVille had been doing. DeVille became **enraged**. He shouted and
glared at Wallace, and demanded that he take back his words. But Wallace
only laughed in his face. We warned Wallace, but it was no use. He laughed
at us the way he laughed at DeVille. Then one day he shoved DeVille's face
into a bucket of glue because DeVille challenged him to fight.

"DeVille was quite a mess—I helped to clean him up. But he was as
cool as a cucumber and made no threat at all. However, I saw a glitter in
his eyes which I had often seen in the eyes of wild beasts. So I went out
of my way to give Wallace a final warning. But he **scoffed** at me and made
light of it all.

"Several months went by. Nothing happened and I was beginning to
think it was all a scare over nothing. By that time we were out West, doing
the show in San Francisco. It was during the afternoon performance and
we were sold out, when I went looking for Red Denny, the assistant manager,
who had walked off with my pocketknife.

"Passing by one of the small tents, I glanced in through a hole in the
canvas to see if I could find him. He wasn't there, but directly in front of
me was King Wallace, in costume, waiting for his turn to go on with his

77

cage of performing lions. Wallace was watching, with amusement, a quarrel between a couple of trapeze artists. All the rest of the people in the tent were watching the same thing. All of them, that is, with the exception of DeVille. I noticed that he was staring at Wallace with a hatred which he did not bother to disguise. Wallace and the rest of them in the tent were all too busy watching the quarrel to notice this or to see what followed.

"But I saw it through a hole in the canvas. DeVille pulled his handkerchief from his pocket and pretended to mop the sweat from his face with it, for it was a hot day. At the same time, he walked past Wallace's back, shaking the handkerchief at him as he passed by. He never stopped, but kept right on going to the doorway. There he turned his head before leaving, and shot a swift glance back at Wallace who had never even seen him. The look troubled me at the time, for I saw not only hatred in it but also triumph.

" 'DeVille will bear watching,' I said to myself. So I breathed easier when I saw him go out the exit to the circus grounds and head for downtown. A few minutes later I was in the big tent, where I had finally caught up with Red Denny. King Wallace was doing his act, holding the audience spellbound. He was in particularly good form, and he kept the lions stirred up till they were all snarling and growling around him—all of them, that is, except Augustus who was just too fat and lazy and old to get upset about anything.

"Finally Wallace slapped the old lion's knees with his whip and got him into position. Old Augustus, blinking good-naturedly, opened his mouth and in popped Wallace's head. Then the jaws came together, *crunch*, just like that."

The Leopard Man smiled in a sweet, sad fashion, and that faraway look came into his eyes.

"And that was the end of King Wallace," he went on in his low, mournful voice. "After the excitement cooled down I watched for my chance and bent over and smelled Wallace's head. Then I sneezed."

"What . . . what was it . . . ?" I asked hesitantly.

"Pepper—that DeVille dropped on Wallace's hair in the tent when he passed by him. Old Augustus never meant to do it. He just couldn't stop himself from sneezing."

SELECTING DETAILS FROM THE STORY.
Each of the following sentences helps
you understand the story. Complete each
sentence below by putting an *x* in the
box next to the correct answer.

1. The Leopard Man thought that his
   job was
   ☐ a. very risky.
   ☐ b. quite interesting.
   ☐ c. not especially exciting.

2. DeVille pinned the ringmaster to the
   backboard with his knives because
   the ringmaster
   ☐ a. insulted DeVille's wife.
   ☐ b. tried to have him fired.
   ☐ c. challenged him to a fight.

3. As he walked past King Wallace's back,
   DeVille
   ☐ a. muttered a threat.
   ☐ b. shook his handkerchief at him.
   ☐ c. grinned wickedly.

4. Old Augustus "crunched down"
   because he
   ☐ a. was ill that day.
   ☐ b. was angry at Wallace.
   ☐ c. couldn't stop himself from
   sneezing.

HANDLING STORY ELEMENTS. Each of
the following questions reviews your
understanding of story elements. Put
an *x* in the box next to the correct
answer to each question.

1. What happened last in the *plot* of
   "The Leopard Man's Story"?
   ☐ a. Wallace shoved DeVille's face
   into a bucket of glue.
   ☐ b. The Leopard Man showed the
   reporter his scars.
   ☐ c. Old Augustus's jaws came
   together with a crunch.

2. Which sentence best *characterizes*
   King Wallace?
   ☐ a. He was not very strong.
   ☐ b. He always listened to advice.
   ☐ c. He was afraid of nothing.

3. Where is "The Leopard Man's
   Story" *set*?
   ☐ a. at a zoo
   ☐ b. at a circus
   ☐ c. in a movie theater

4. Which sentence best tells the *theme* of
   the story?
   ☐ a. A circus performer gets revenge
   on the man he hates.
   ☐ b. A reporter attempts to find an
   interesting story.
   ☐ c. Circus animals are dangerous
   on occasion.

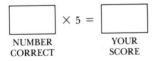

NUMBER   YOUR
CORRECT   SCORE

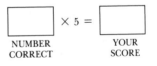

NUMBER   YOUR
CORRECT   SCORE

OBSERVING NEW VOCABULARY WORDS. Answer the following vocabulary questions by putting an *x* in the box next to the correct answer. The vocabulary words are printed in **boldface** in the story. If you wish, look back at the words before you answer the questions.

1. When Wallace made fun of DeVille, he became enraged and shouted at Wallace. The word *enraged* means
   ☐ a. furious.
   ☐ b. curious.
   ☐ c. shy.

2. The Leopard Man warned Wallace, but the lion tamer scoffed at him and made light of it. The word *scoffed* means
   ☐ a. took seriously.
   ☐ b. made fun of.
   ☐ c. attacked.

3. The Leopard Man did not think there were terrible perils in his work; he did not find it thrilling. As used here, the word *perils* means
   ☐ a. dangers.
   ☐ b. deeds.
   ☐ c. audiences.

4. When the lion changed his tactics and charged with his head down, the lion tamer stuck out his leg. What is the meaning of the word *tactics?*
   ☐ a. hours or times
   ☐ b. owners or masters
   ☐ c. methods or ways of doing things

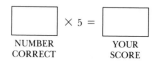

NUMBER CORRECT   × 5 =   YOUR SCORE

COMPLETING A CLOZE PASSAGE. Complete the following paragraph by filling in each blank with one of the words listed in the box below. Each of the words appears in the story. Since there are five words and four blanks, one word in the group will not be used.

At a three ring circus, there's

_____ more to see than the
1

eye can follow. Should you concentrate

on the acrobats or the _____
2

artists? Should you watch the clowns and

the jugglers, the lion _____,
3

or the trained animals? So much is

happening all at once that it's impossible

to pay _____ to everything.
4

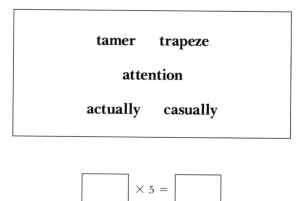

tamer	trapeze
attention	
actually	**casually**

NUMBER CORRECT   × 5 =   YOUR SCORE

KNOWING HOW TO READ CRITICALLY. Each of the following questions will help you to think critically about the selection. Put an *x* in the box next to the correct answer.

1. Evidence in the story indicates that DeVille
   - ☐ a. was a very calm person.
   - ☐ b. seldom got into fights.
   - ☐ c. had a fierce temper.

2. Which statement is true?
   - ☐ a. DeVille must have sprinkled some pepper on his handkerchief.
   - ☐ b. In a fair fight, DeVille would surely have easily defeated Wallace.
   - ☐ c. For months, Wallace was very worried about what DeVille might do.

3. We may infer that DeVille
   - ☐ a. had nothing to do with Wallace's accidental death.
   - ☐ b. had quietly been planning Wallace's death.
   - ☐ c. felt sad when he heard about Wallace's death.

4. It is fair to say that Wallace should have
   - ☐ a. realized that Old Augustus couldn't be trusted.
   - ☐ b. put his head into the mouth of one of the other lions.
   - ☐ c. taken the Leopard Man's warning very seriously.

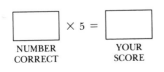

NUMBER CORRECT   × 5 =   YOUR SCORE

Questions for Writing and Discussion

- Before he left the circus grounds, DeVille cast a swift glance at Wallace. The look showed hatred as well as triumph. Explain DeVille's look.
- Why do you think DeVille chose not to be present when Old Augustus "crunched down"? What do you think DeVille said when he heard about what happened?
- Why did DeVille's plan require a hot day? Do you believe DeVille got away with the crime? Explain your answers.

Use the boxes below to total your scores for the exercises. Then write your score on pages 150 and 151.

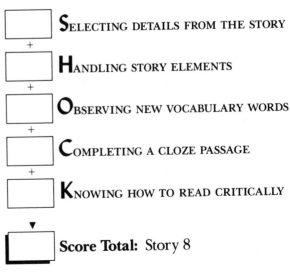

SELECTING DETAILS FROM THE STORY

+

HANDLING STORY ELEMENTS

+

OBSERVING NEW VOCABULARY WORDS

+

COMPLETING A CLOZE PASSAGE

+

KNOWING HOW TO READ CRITICALLY

▼

Score Total: Story 8

9

The Story of an Hour

by Kate Chopin

$\mathcal{E}$veryone knew that Louise Mallard suffered from heart trouble. There-fore, great care was taken to break the news of her husband's death as gently as possible to her.

It was her sister Josephine who told her. She revealed the news slowly, in broken sentences and hints. Her husband's friend, Richards, was there, too. It was he who had been in the newspaper office when word of the terrible railroad accident was received. Brently Mallard's name was at the top of the list of "killed." Richards had quickly sent a telegram to **confirm** the facts. Then he hurried to Mrs. Mallard's house. He wanted to make sure he arrived before some less caring friend delivered the sad message.

When Mrs. Mallard heard the story, she grasped at once what had happened. She wept suddenly, wildly, in her sister's arms. When the storm of grief finally spent itself, she went to her room alone. She would let no one follow her.

In front of the open window in her room stood a large, comfortable armchair. Into this she sank with exhaustion. She felt pressed down by a weariness that haunted her body and seemed to reach into her soul.

She looked out the window. In the open square in front of her house she could see the tops of trees. They were fluttering with new spring life. The sweet, fresh smell of rain was in the air. In the street below, she heard a peddler selling his **wares**. In the distance, someone was singing a song— the notes faintly reached her ears. She could hear, too, the twittering of countless birds on the roof.

Patches of blue sky showed here and there. They burst through the billowing clouds in the west facing her window.

She sat with her head thrown back on the cushion of the chair. She did not move at all, except when a sob came up into her throat and shook her. She was like a child who has cried itself to sleep and continues to sob in its dreams.

She was young with a fair, calm face. The few lines there suggested a certain strength. But now there was a dull stare in her eyes. Her gaze was fixed far off in the distance—on one of those patches of blue sky. She did not seem to be thinking of anything. No. She did not seem to be thinking of anything at all. She seemed to be waiting, waiting . . .

There was something coming to her. And she was waiting for it. Waiting fearfully. What was it? She did not know. It was something too **subtle**, too new and strange. But she felt it. She felt it creeping out of the sky. It was reaching toward her through the sounds, the smells, the colors that filled the air.

Now her heart began to pound wildly. She was beginning to recognize this thing, this feeling that was coming to possess her. At the same time, she was trying to beat back this feeling. She was trying to beat it back with her will. But her will was powerless to do so.

When she finally let herself go, one little whispered word escaped from her lips. She said it over and over under her breath. "Free. Free. *Free.*"

The blank stare and the look of terror that had followed it left her eyes. They became clear and bright. Her heart beat fast. The rushing blood warmed and relaxed every inch of her body.

Was it some terrible, some **monstrous** joy that now gripped her? She did not stop to ask. Something told her that the question was not important.

She knew that she would weep again. She would weep when she saw her husband's kind, tender hands folded in death. When she saw his face—which had never looked at her except with love— staring, gray and dead. But she saw beyond that bitter moment. She saw the long line of years to come, years that would belong only to her—to herself completely. And she spread her arms out to them in welcome.

There would be no one to live *for* during those years to come. She would live for herself! And yet she had loved Brently—sometimes. Often she had not. What did it matter! What could love, the unsolved mystery, count for in the face of this sense of freedom she suddenly felt—this powerful emotion which had taken possession of her.

"Free! Body and soul free!" she kept whispering.

Josephine was kneeling outside the closed door. She had her mouth to the keyhole, begging to be admitted.

"Louise, open the door! I beg you, open the door! You'll make yourself ill. What are you doing? Please, open the door."

"Go away," Louise said. "I am not making myself ill."

No, she was drinking in life—life itself—through that open window.

Her imagination was running wild as she thought of those days ahead. Spring days, and summer days, and all sorts of days that would be hers

alone. She breathed a quick prayer that life might be long. It was only yesterday that she thought, with a shudder, that life might be long.

She stood up, finally, and opened the door to her sister. There was triumph in her eyes, and she carried herself like a goddess of Victory. She put her arm around her sister, and together they went down the stairs. Richards stood waiting for them at the bottom.

Someone was entering the front door with a key.

It was Brently Mallard who entered.

He was calmly carrying his suitcase and umbrella. He had been far away from the scene of the accident and did not even know there had been one. He stood there amazed when Josephine saw him and screamed. He was surprised as Richards quickly moved to shield him from his wife.

But Richards was too late.

When the doctors came, they said she had died of a heart attack—of joy that kills.

SELECTING DETAILS FROM THE STORY.
Each of the following sentences helps
you understand the story. Complete each
sentence below by putting an *x* in the
box next to the correct answer.

1. When Louise Mallard heard that her
   husband had died, she
   ☐ a. wept and went to her room.
   ☐ b. became dizzy and passed out.
   ☐ c. refused to believe it.

2. After a while, Louise realized that
   she was
   ☐ a. all alone in the world.
   ☐ b. free to live for herself.
   ☐ c. too poor to enjoy life.

3. Louise's imagination ran wild as she
   thought about
   ☐ a. the terrible accident.
   ☐ b. the vacation she had planned.
   ☐ c. all the days ahead of her.

4. When Brently Mallard entered the
   room, Richards tried to
   ☐ a. rush him out of the room.
   ☐ b. tell Louise the good news.
   ☐ c. shield him from his wife.

HANDLING STORY ELEMENTS. Each of
the following questions reviews your
understanding of story elements. Put
an *x* in the box next to the correct
answer to each question.

1. What happened last in the *plot* of
   "The Story of an Hour"?
   ☐ a. Josephine saw Brently Mallard
        and screamed.
   ☐ b. Josephine told her sister the
        bad news.
   ☐ c. Louise and Josephine came down
        the stairs together.

2. Who is the *main character* in the story?
   ☐ a. Louise Mallard
   ☐ b. Brently Mallard
   ☐ c. Josephine

3. What is the *setting* of the story?
   ☐ a. a newspaper office one winter
   ☐ b. the Mallard house one spring
   ☐ c. a railroad office one summer

4. In "The Story of an Hour," Louise
   experienced *conflict* as she struggled
   to deal with
   ☐ a. whether or not to move away.
   ☐ b. how to tell her friends and family
        about Brently's death.
   ☐ c. the love she felt for her husband
        and her new sense of freedom.

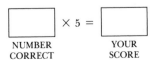

NUMBER   YOUR
CORRECT   SCORE

× 5 =

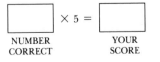

NUMBER   YOUR
CORRECT   SCORE

× 5 =

OBSERVING NEW VOCABULARY WORDS. Answer the following vocabulary questions by putting an *x* in the box next to the correct answer. The vocabulary words are printed in **boldface** in the story. If you wish, look back at the words before you answer the questions.

1. Mrs. Mallard heard a peddler in the street selling his wares. Which of the following best defines the word *wares*?
   ☐ a. valuable information
   ☐ b. enjoyable songs
   ☐ c. articles for sale

2. She wondered if it was some terrible, some monstrous joy that gripped her. What is the meaning of the word *monstrous*?
   ☐ a. horrible
   ☐ b. unusual
   ☐ c. tiny

3. When he learned that Brently had been killed, Richards sent a telegram to confirm the facts. The word *confirm* means to
   ☐ a. change.
   ☐ b. make certain of.
   ☐ c. remove.

4. She could not tell what the feeling was—it was too subtle, too new and strange. Something that is *subtle* is
   ☐ a. very clear.
   ☐ b. very foolish.
   ☐ c. not obvious.

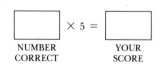

NUMBER   YOUR
CORRECT   SCORE

COMPLETING A CLOZE PASSAGE. Complete the following paragraph by filling in each blank with one of the words listed in the box below. Each of the words appears in the story. Since there are five words and four blanks, one word in the group will not be used.

The first _____ railroad in
                            ₁

the United States was the Baltimore &

Ohio. This _____ began
                     ₂

operating out of Baltimore, Maryland,

in 1830. The train that moved

_____ along the first section
              ₃

of track was pulled by horses. Later, of

course, the trains were _____
                                    ₄

by steam.

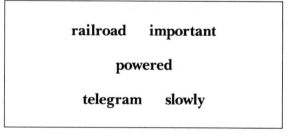

railroad   important

powered

telegram   slowly

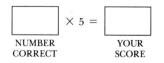

NUMBER   YOUR
CORRECT   SCORE

KNOWING HOW TO READ CRITICALLY. Each of the following questions will help you to think critically about the selection. Put an *x* in the box next to the correct answer.

1. Why did Josephine tell her sister the bad news "slowly, in broken sentences and hints"?
   ☐ a. Josephine was very confused about how Brently died.
   ☐ b. Josephine didn't speak very well.
   ☐ c. Josephine was trying to break the news to her sister gently.

2. It was only yesterday that Louise "thought, with a shudder, that life might be long." This suggests Louise was
   ☐ a. happy.
   ☐ b. unhappy.
   ☐ c. very busy.

3. Louise was "drinking in life" through the open window. This means that Louise was beginning to
   ☐ a. feel sorry for herself.
   ☐ b. retreat, or draw back, from life.
   ☐ c. truly become aware of the world around her.

4. Why did Richards attempt to shield Brently from his wife?
   ☐ a. Richards was afraid that Louise would be shocked.
   ☐ b. Richards was planning to surprise Louise later.
   ☐ c. Richards wanted to ask Brently where he had been.

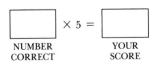

	× 5 =	
NUMBER CORRECT		YOUR SCORE

Questions for Writing and Discussion
- The doctors said that Louise died "of joy that kills." Do you believe they were right? What do you think went through Louise's mind when she saw her husband?
- When Louise finally went to open the door to her sister, "there was triumph in her eyes, and she carried herself like a goddess of Victory." Explain why Louise looked and felt that way.
- "The Story of an Hour" was written more than a hundred years ago. Does that surprise you? Explain why.

Use the boxes below to total your scores for the exercises. Then write your score on pages 150 and 151.

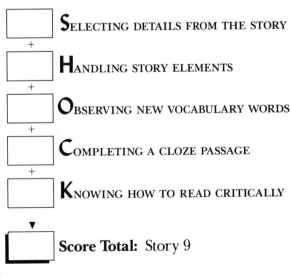

SELECTING DETAILS FROM THE STORY

+

HANDLING STORY ELEMENTS

+

OBSERVING NEW VOCABULARY WORDS

+

COMPLETING A CLOZE PASSAGE

+

KNOWING HOW TO READ CRITICALLY

▼

Score Total: Story 9

10

Anansi's Fishing Trip

A TALE FROM GHANA

*I*n the country of Ashanti, not far from the edge of the great West African forest, there was a man named Anansi, who was known to all the people for miles around. Anansi was not a great hunter or a great worker or a great warrior. His specialty was being clever. He liked to outwit people. He liked to live well and to have other people do things for him. But because all the people of the country knew about Anansi and had had trouble with him, he had to keep thinking of new ways to get something for nothing.

One day Anansi was sitting in the village when a man named Osansa came along.

"I have an idea," Anansi said. "Why don't we go and set fish traps together? Then we shall sell the fish and be quite rich."

But Osansa knew Anansi's reputation very well, and so he said, "No, I have as much food as I can eat or sell. I am rich enough. Why don't you set your fish traps by yourself?"

"Ha! Fish alone? Then I'd have to do all the work!" Anansi said. "What I need is a fool for a partner."

Osansa went away, and after a while another man named Anene came along.

"I have an idea," Anansi said. "Why don't the two of us go and set fish traps together? Then we shall sell the fish and be quite rich."

Anene knew Anansi very well too, but he seemed to listen thoughtfully.

91

"That sounds like a fine idea," he said. "Two people can catch more fish than one. Yes, I'll do it."

The news went rapidly around the village that Anansi and Anene were going on a fishing expedition together. Osansa met Anene in the market and said, "We hear you are going to trap fish with Anansi. Don't you know he is trying to make a fool of you? He has told everyone that he needs a fool to go fishing with him. He wants someone to set the fish traps and do all the work, while he gets all the money for the fish."

"Don't worry, friend Osansa, I won't be Anansi's fool," Anene said.

Early the next morning Anansi and Anene went into the woods to cut palm branches to make their fish traps.

Anansi was busy thinking how he could make Anene do most of the work. But when they came to the place where the palm trees grew, Anene said to Anansi, "Give me the knife, Anansi. I shall cut the branches for the traps. We are partners. We share everything. My part of the work will be to cut branches, your part of the work will be to get tired for me."

"Just a minute, let me think," Anansi said. "Why should I be the one to get tired?"

"Well, when there's work to be done someone must get tired," Anene said. "That's the way it is. So if I cut the branches, the least you can do is to get tired for me."

"Hah, you take me for a fool?" Anansi said. "Give me the knife. I shall cut the branches, and you get tired for me!"

So Anansi took the knife and began cutting the branches from the trees. Every time he chopped, Anene grunted. Anene sat down in the shade and groaned from weariness, while Anansi chopped and hacked and sweated. Finally the wood for the fish traps was cut. Anansi tied it up into a big bundle. Anene got up from the ground, holding his back and moaning.

"Anansi, let me carry the bundle of wood now, and you can get tired for me," Anene said.

"Oh, no, my friend Anene," Anansi said, "I am not that simpleminded. I'll carry the wood myself, and you can take the weariness for me."

So he **hoisted** the bundle to the top of his head, and the two of them started back to the village. Anene groaned all the way.

"Oh, oh!" he moaned. "Take it easy, Anansi! Oh, oh!"

When they came to the village, Anene said, "Let me make the fish traps, Anansi, and you just sit down and get tired for me."

"Oh, no," Anansi said. "You just keep on as you are." And he made the fish traps while Anene lay on his back in the shade with his eyes closed, moaning and groaning.

And while he was making the traps, working in the heat with perspiration running down his face and chest, Anansi looked at Anene lying there taking all his weariness and sore muscles for him, and he shook his head and clucked his tongue.

"Anene thinks he is intelligent," he said to himself. "Yet look at him moaning and groaning there, practically dying from weariness!"

When the fish traps were done, Anene climbed to his feet and said, "Anansi, my friend, now let me carry the fish traps to the water, and you can get tired for me."

"Oh, no," Anansi said. "You just come along and do your share. I'll do the carrying, you do the getting tired."

So they went down to the water, Anansi carrying and Anene moaning. When they arrived, Anene said to Anansi, "Now wait a minute, Anansi, we ought to think things over here. There are sharks in this water. Someone is **apt** to get hurt. So let me go in and set the traps, and should a shark bite me, then you can die for me."

"Wah!" Anansi howled. "Listen to that! What do you take me for? I'll go in the water and set the traps myself, and if I am bitten, then you can die for me!" So he took the fish traps out into the water and set them, and then the two of them went back to the village.

The next morning when they went down to inspect the traps, they found just four fish. Anene spoke first.

"Anansi, there are only four fish here. You take them. Tomorrow there will probably be more, and then I'll take my turn."

"Now, what do you take me for?" Anansi said indignantly. "Do you think I am simpleminded? Oh, no, Anene, you take the four fish, and I'll take my turn tomorrow."

So Anene took the four fish and carried them to town and sold them.

Next day when they came down to the fish traps, Anene said, "Look, there are only eight fish here. I'm glad it's your turn, because tomorrow there doubtless will be more."

"Just a minute," Anansi said. "You want me to take today's fish so that tomorrow you get a bigger catch? Oh, no, they are all yours, partner; tomorrow I'll take my share."

So Anene took the eight fish and carried them to town and sold them.

Next day when they came to look in the traps they found sixteen fish.

"Anansi," Anene said, "take the sixteen fish. Little ones, too. I'll take my turn tomorrow."

"Of course you'll take your turn tomorrow, it's my turn today," Anansi said. He stopped to think. "Well, now, you are trying to make a fool out of me again! You want me to take these sixteen miserable little fish so that you can get the big catch tomorrow, don't you? Well, it's a good thing I'm alert! You take the sixteen today, and I'll take the big catch tomorrow!"

So Anene carried the sixteen fish to the market and sold them.

Next day they came to the traps and took the fish out. But by this time the traps had rotted in the water.

"Well, it's certainly your turn today," Anene said. "And I'm very glad of that. Look, the fish traps are rotten and worn out. We can't use them any more. I'll tell you what—you take the fish to town and sell them, and I'll take the rotten fish traps and sell them. The fish traps will bring an excellent price. What a wonderful idea!"

"Hm," Anansi said. "Just a moment, don't be in such a hurry. I'll take the fish traps and sell them myself. If there's such a good price to be had, why shouldn't I get it instead of you? Oh, no, you take the fish, my friend."

Anansi hoisted the rotten fish traps up on his head and started off for town. Anene followed him, carrying the fish. When they arrived in the town, Anene sold his fish in the market, while Anansi walked back and forth singing loudly, "I am selling rotten fish traps! I am selling wonderful rotten fish traps!"

But no one wanted rotten fish traps, and the townspeople were angry that Anansi thought they were so stupid they would buy them. All day long Anansi wandered through the town singing, "Get your rotten fish traps here! I am selling wonderful rotten fish traps!"

Finally the head man of the town heard about the affair. He, too, became very angry, and he sent messengers for Anansi. When they brought Anansi to him he asked indignantly, "What do you think you are doing, anyway? What kind of nonsense is this you are trying to put over on the people of the town?"

"I'm selling rotten fish traps," Anansi said, "very excellent rotten fish traps."

"Now what do you take us for?" the chief of the town said. "Do you think we are **ignorant** people? Your friend Anene came and sold good fish, which the people want, but you come trying to sell something that isn't good for anything and just smell the town up with your rotten fish traps. It's an outrage. You insult us."

The head man turned to the townspeople who stood nearby, listening.

"Take him away and whip him," he said.

The men took Anansi out to the town gate and beat him with sticks. Anansi shouted and yelled and made a great noise. When at last they turned him loose, Anene said to him, "Anansi, this ought to be a lesson to you. You wanted a fool to go fishing with you, but you didn't have to look so hard to find one. You were a fool yourself."

"Yes," he said thoughtfully, rubbing his back and his legs where they had beaten him. And he looked **reproachfully** at Anene. "But what kind of partner are you? At least you could have taken the pain while I took the beating."

SELECTING DETAILS FROM THE STORY.
Each of the following sentences helps
you understand the story. Complete each
sentence below by putting an *x* in the
box next to the correct answer.

1. At the beginning of the story, Anansi
   was looking for
   ☐ a. a fool to be his partner.
   ☐ b. a friend who owned a fishing
   boat.
   ☐ c. someone to lend him money.

2. Anansi decided that he would do the
   work while Anene
   ☐ a. paid him.
   ☐ b. learned from him.
   ☐ c. got tired for him.

3. When Anene offered to set the traps
   in the water, Anansi
   ☐ a. agreed to let him do that.
   ☐ b. insisted on setting them himself.
   ☐ c. thanked Anene for making the
   suggestion.

4. The chief ordered the townspeople to
   ☐ a. whip Anansi.
   ☐ b. insult Anansi.
   ☐ c. buy some fish traps from Anansi.

HANDLING STORY ELEMENTS. Each of
the following questions reviews your
understanding of story elements. Put
an *x* in the box next to the correct
answer to each question.

1. What happened last in the *plot* of
   "Anansi's Fishing Trip"?
   ☐ a. The men beat Anansi with sticks.
   ☐ b. Anansi walked back and forth
   calling, "I am selling wonderful
   rotten fish traps."
   ☐ c. Anene offered Anansi sixteen
   little fish.

2. Which sentence best *characterizes* Anansi?
   ☐ a. He was a great hunter.
   ☐ b. He was a great warrior.
   ☐ c. He tried to get something for
   nothing by outwitting people.

3. The *mood* of "Anansi's Fishing Trip"
   may best be described as
   ☐ a. light and amusing.
   ☐ b. sad or sorrowful.
   ☐ c. terrifying or frightening.

4. Which of the following best tells the
   theme of the story?
   ☐ a. A man tries to sell rotten fish
   traps that nobody wants.
   ☐ b. A man decides to turn the tables
   on someone who is trying to
   trick him.
   ☐ c. A man gives up his share of fish
   in the hope of obtaining a larger
   share later.

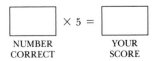

NUMBER   YOUR
CORRECT   SCORE

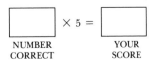

NUMBER   YOUR
CORRECT   SCORE

OBSERVING NEW VOCABULARY WORDS.
Answer the following vocabulary questions by putting an *x* in the box next to the correct answer. The vocabulary words are printed in **boldface** in the story. If you wish, look back at the words before you answer the questions.

1. Anansi hoisted the bundle to the top of his head. The word *hoisted* means
   ☐ a. dropped.
   ☐ b. lifted high.
   ☐ c. broke into pieces.

2. The chief said that only ignorant people would buy rotten fish traps. Someone who is *ignorant*
   ☐ a. knows little or nothing.
   ☐ b. has a great deal of knowledge.
   ☐ c. makes wise decisions.

3. Since there were sharks in the water, someone was apt to get hurt. As used here, the word *apt* means
   ☐ a. lucky.
   ☐ b. likely.
   ☐ c. lazy.

4. Anansi looked reproachfully at Anene and accused him of being a bad partner. When you act *reproachfully,* you
   ☐ a. praise someone.
   ☐ b. help someone.
   ☐ c. blame someone.

COMPLETING A CLOZE PASSAGE. Complete the following paragraph by filling in each blank with one of the words listed in the box below. Each of the words appears in the story. Since there are five words and four blanks, one word in the group will not be used.

In the southwestern part of

_____ , beyond a broad
    1

plain, lies a wide forest plateau.

This is _____ as the great
            2

West African forest. Miles of tall, dense

_____ stretch as far as the eye
        3

can see. This huge forest serves as an

_____ home to hundreds of
        4

various plants and animals.

excellent	**known**
Ghana	
trees	**warrior**

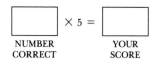

NUMBER   YOUR
CORRECT   SCORE

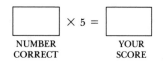

NUMBER   YOUR
CORRECT   SCORE

KNOWING HOW TO READ CRITICALLY. Each of the following questions will help you to think critically about the selection. Put an *x* in the box next to the correct answer.

1. The story demonstrates that Anansi was
   □ a. smarter than anyone in town.
   □ b. not as clever as he thought he was.
   □ c. able to fool Anene.

2. We may infer that Anene
   □ a. pretended to be weary and exhausted.
   □ b. got so tired he could hardly move.
   □ c. was afraid that Anansi was going to fool him.

3. Which statement is true?
   □ a. Anansi had an excellent reputation.
   □ b. The head man of the town was amused by Anansi's actions.
   □ c. Anene profited from Anansi's labor.

4. It is fair to say that Anene knew that Anansi would
   □ a. act in a fair and honest way.
   □ b. accept all of his suggestions.
   □ c. do the opposite of whatever Anene suggested.

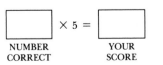

NUMBER
CORRECT   × 5 =   YOUR
SCORE

Questions for Writing and Discussion

- Anene stated that he wanted to teach Anansi a lesson. Did Anene succeed in doing that? Explain your answer.
- Anansi was defeated by his lack of trust in other people. Find examples from the story to prove that statement.
- Suppose that Anene has offered to repair the rotten fish traps. What do you think Anansi would have done? Anansi wanted a fool to go fishing with him. Anene suggested that Anansi found that fool. Who was it?

Use the boxes below to total your scores for the exercises. Then write your score on pages 150 and 151.

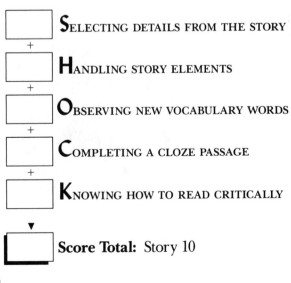

SELECTING DETAILS FROM THE STORY

+

HANDLING STORY ELEMENTS

+

OBSERVING NEW VOCABULARY WORDS

+

COMPLETING A CLOZE PASSAGE

+

KNOWING HOW TO READ CRITICALLY

▼

Score Total: Story 10

II

A Lodging for the Night

by Lin Yutang

*W*hen Li Tsing, the great general, was still an unknown young man, he used to hunt in the Huo Mountains. He was a familiar sight among the villagers in that mountainous region. Because he had such a winning personality and was so friendly to everybody, they liked him very much.

On his hunting trips, he often stopped at a certain village for supper or lunch. There was an elder of that village who always gave him food and shelter whenever he was out late and could not get back to the city. The elder was wealthy and would never accept any payment. He always provided a hot supper and lodging for the night for Li Tsing.

One day, on one of his hunting trips, Li sighted a herd of deer and started to follow their track. He was a good horseman and rode swiftly over hill and dale, following the tracks to the top of a hill where he hoped to sight the herd again. But the deer had somehow completely eluded him; he could not find them.

Li was too determined a hunter to give up. Therefore, he crossed over hill after hill in an attempt to find them, and by the time it was pitch dark he did not know where he was. Upset and tired, he tried to find his way back, but the land was unfamiliar to him. Soon he was delighted to see a light shining from the top of a mountain opposite him. He was sure he could reach it in half an hour, and he headed in that direction, hoping to find a lodging for the night.

Arriving at the place, Li found a mansion enclosed by a high white wall with a red gate. He knocked and waited. After a long while, a servant came to open the side door and asked what he wanted. Li told him that he had been out hunting and had lost his way, and he begged their hospitality.

"I am afraid it is impossible," said the servant. "The men are away and only the lady of the house is at home."

"Will you please speak to the lady for me anyway?"

The servant went inside and soon returned, saying, "Come in. The lady was at first unwilling to accept you as a guest. But on hearing that you had lost your way, she thought about it again and said that she would let you have a room for the night."

Li was ushered into the hall, which was elegantly furnished with many crystal lamps and plates and other fine objects. Shortly afterward, the lady of the house appeared. She was very dignified, over fifty, dressed simply in black. Li noticed that everything she wore was of the finest material. He bowed and apologized for having arrived so unexpectedly.

"My sons are away tonight," she said, "and ordinarily I would not receive guests. However, you are lost on such a dark night that I have not the heart to send you away." She spoke with great poise, and her tone and manner were that of the kindly mother of a happy, well-run family. Even her graying hair was beautiful.

Li was served a simple, excellent supper, which consisted mainly of fish. He ate with ivory chopsticks from beautiful crystal bowls.

After supper, the lady excused herself, saying to him, "You must be tired and will want to retire for the night at once. My servants shall see that you have everything."

Li rose to thank her and said goodnight.

The lady said goodnight and added, "It may be noisy at night. I hope that will not disturb you."

Li's eyes registered surprise, and she noticed it.

"My boys often come back in the middle of the night and make much noise," explained the lady. "I just wanted to let you know so that you would not be frightened.

"I shall not be frightened," said Li. He wanted to know how old her boys were and what they were doing, but he thought it best not to act too curious.

Two servants soon brought out a roll of fine clean bedding to make his bed, and having seen that he had everything, they went out and closed the door.

It was a comfortable, warm bed, and he was tired after the day's hunt. But he wondered what kind of people he was stopping with. What kind of people lived so far away from everything and had business at night? His limbs were exhausted and ready for a good sleep, but his mind was fully awake. Like a hunter stalking his prey, he lay perfectly still in bed, waiting to hear what might happen.

Toward midnight, he heard a loud and urgent knock at the gate. Soon he heard the creak of the side door, and the servant talking to someone in whispers. Then he heard the servant's steps coming to the parlor, and he heard the lady come out.

"What is it?" she asked the servant.

"The messenger brought this scroll. He says it is urgent," replied the servant. "The **scroll** says that one of your sons is ordered to make it rain in this region for seven miles around the mountain, but the rain is to stop before dawn. There must not be too much rain, for fear of hurting the crops."

"What can I do?" said the lady in a low, worried voice. "Both of my sons are away and it is too late to send for them. I cannot send anybody else."

"Can you ask our guest to do it?" suggested a servant. "He is a strong fellow and a hunter. He rides a horse well."

The lady was delighted with the suggestion and came to knock at Li's door. "Are you awake?" she called.

Li answered, "What can I do for you?"

"Please come out. I have something to talk over with you."

Li got out of bed at once and came out into the parlor. The lady explained, "This is not an ordinary house. You are stopping at the Dragon's **residence**. I have received an order from Heaven to make rain at once, between now and dawn, and I have nobody to send. My eldest son is away attending a wedding in the Eastern Sea, and my second boy has accompanied his younger sister on a distant journey. They are thousands of miles away, and it is too late to send a message to them. Will you be so kind as to take the job? Making rains is our duty, and my sons will be punished if this order is not obeyed."

Li was astonished by such an amazing request. "I would be glad to oblige," he said, "but it is beyond my power and experience. I suppose one must fly up above the clouds to make rain."

"You can ride a horse well, I presume."

"Certainly."

"That is enough," said the lady. All you need to do is mount the horse I shall give you—not your own horse, of course—and follow my instructions. It is quite simple."

She ordered a black-maned horse to be brought and saddled. Then she handed Li a small bottle containing rainwater, which was to be hung in front of the saddle.

"This is a celestial—a heavenly—horse," she said. "You must hold the reins lightly and let him trot wherever he likes. Do not hurry him. He knows where to go. Whenever you see him paw with his hoofs, just take this bottle and sprinkle *one* drop of water below. But be careful not to sprinkle too much. Do not forget."

Li climbed on the celestial horse and set off. He was surprised at its steadiness and speed. Soon it trotted a little faster but maintained an even pace. Li had a feeling that he was rising. As he looked about, he saw that he was already on top of the clouds. A swift, moist wind blew fiercely against his face, and below him thunder rolled and lightning flashed. Following the instructions, he sprinkled a drop of the divine water whenever the horse stopped and pawed.

After a while, with the help of flashes of lightning, he looked through an opening in the clouds and saw the village where he often used to stop for the night.

"I have bothered the old man and these villagers a great deal," he thought to himself. "For years I have been wanting to repay them for their hospitality, and now I have the power to make it rain. Yesterday I saw that their crops were **parched** on the field, drooping and yellowing. I will sprinkle a little more for those nice people."

He sprinkled twenty drops on the village and felt happy as he watched the rain pour down. When it was over, he returned to the Dragon's home.

The lady of the house was weeping in a chair in the parlor.

"What a terrible blunder you have made!" she cried when she saw him return. "I told you to sprinkle one drop of water, and you must have poured down half a bottle. You did not know that one drop of that liquid means one foot of rainfall on earth. How many drops did you sprinkle?"

"Only twenty," Li replied, feeling very foolish.

"*Only* twenty! Can you imagine a village suddenly flooded with twenty feet of rain in one night! All the people and cattle will be drowned. Of course a report will be made to heaven, and my sons will be held responsible for this disaster."

Li was ashamed of himself and did not know what to say except that he was very sorry. But of course it was too late.

"I do not blame you," said the lady. "You could not have known. But I am afraid that when the Dragon comes home, it will not be pleasant for you. I advise you to leave immediately."

Li was touched by the lady's kindness and prepared to leave at once. It was already daybreak. He was glad to get away so easily, but to his surprise the lady said to him when he was all ready to go, "I must repay you for the trouble you took. I should not have asked a guest to get up in the middle of the night. It was my fault. Out here I have no costly gifts to give you, but I can furnish you with two servants. You can take either of them or both, whatever you wish."

Li looked at the two servants standing on either side of the lady. The one on the east looked gentle and kind. The one on the west looked tough, powerful, and fierce.

Li thought he could use a servant, and he wanted to have a living remembrance of that strange night's visit.

"I will take one servant," he said.

"As you like," said the lady. "Make your choice."

Li paused and considered. The gentle servant on the east looked intelligent and friendly. But he might not be a very useful companion on a hunting trip. Li said he would take the one on the west—the strong fellow with the rather savage-looking appearance.

He thanked his hostess and left. He turned around to look at the house once more and saw that it had disappeared. When he turned back to question the servant, he too was gone.

Li found his way back home alone. On reaching the spot where the village had stood, he saw a huge flood covering everything except the tallest treetops. All inhabitants had been drowned during the night!

Later, Li became a great general. He led many victorious battles which ended in the founding of the T'ang Dynasty. But through the long years of his service to the Emperor, who was his close friend, he never became a governor of the people of China. This is because he had not chosen the gentle servant.

There is a **proverb** that good generals come from the western part of the country and good governors from the eastern part. He had chosen the servant on the west side of the lady. He had therefore become a famous general. Had he chosen both servants, he would have become a great governor as well as a great general.

SELECTING DETAILS FROM THE STORY.
Each of the following sentences helps you understand the story. Complete each sentence below by putting an *x* in the box next to the correct answer.

1. One day, while he was on a hunting trip, Li Tsing
   ☐ a. fell and injured himself.
   ☐ b. was attacked by robbers.
   ☐ c. became lost.

2. The lady of the house told Li that her sons
   ☐ a. were excellent hunters.
   ☐ b. would be home in the morning.
   ☐ c. were thousands of miles away.

3. Li was very sorry that he had
   ☐ a. refused the lady's request for help.
   ☐ b. sprinkled 20 drops of water on the village.
   ☐ c. failed to become a great general.

4. At the end of the story, Li accepted the lady's offer and decided to take
   ☐ a. one servant.
   ☐ b. both servants.
   ☐ c. several costly gifts.

HANDLING STORY ELEMENTS. Each of the following questions reviews your understanding of story elements. Put an *x* in the box next to the correct answer to each question.

1. What happened first in the *plot* of "A Lodging for the Night"?
   ☐ a. Li Tsing saw that a huge flood had drowned everyone in the village.
   ☐ b. The servant told Li that it was not possible for him to enter the house.
   ☐ c. Li realized that he was riding on top of the clouds.

2. Which sentence best *characterizes* the lady of the house?
   ☐ a. She was about twenty years old, and wore elegant clothing.
   ☐ b. She was thirty years old, stubborn, and thoughtless.
   ☐ c. She was over fifty, well spoken, and kindly.

3. "When you see him paw with his hoofs, just take this bottle and sprinkle one drop of water below." That line of *dialogue* was spoken by
   ☐ a. Li Tsing.
   ☐ b. the lady of the house.
   ☐ c. a servant.

4. "A Loding for the Night" is *set*
   ☐ a. in China, long ago.
   ☐ b. somewhere in the United States.
   ☐ c. in England.

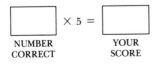

☐ × 5 = ☐

NUMBER   YOUR
CORRECT   SCORE

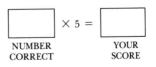

☐ × 5 = ☐

NUMBER   YOUR
CORRECT   SCORE

OBSERVING NEW VOCABULARY WORDS. Answer the following vocabulary questions by putting an *x* in the box next to the correct answer. The vocabulary words are printed in **boldface** in the story. If you wish, look back at the words before you answer the questions.

1. The scroll said that one of the sons was ordered to make it rain. A *scroll* is
   ☐ a. an expensive present.
   ☐ b. a small, shiny radio.
   ☐ c. a roll of paper with writing on it.

2. The lady explained that it was not an ordinary house—it was the Dragon's residence. The word *residence* means
   ☐ a. home.
   ☐ b. business.
   ☐ c. knowledge.

3. Because it had not rained, the crops were parched and were turning yellow. What is the meaning of the word *parched*?
   ☐ a. blooming
   ☐ b. planted
   ☐ c. dried out

4. There is a proverb that good generals come from the western part of the country and good governors from the eastern part. What is a *proverb*?
   ☐ a. a puzzle
   ☐ b. an old saying
   ☐ c. an important letter

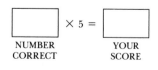

NUMBER
CORRECT

YOUR
SCORE

COMPLETING A CLOZE PASSAGE. Complete the following paragraph by filling in each blank with one of the words listed in the box below. Each of the words appears in the story. Since there are five words and four blanks, one word in the group will not be used.

From the beginning of the seventh century to the beginning of the tenth century, _____ thrived under the T'ang Dynasty. _____ emperors supported art, poetry, music, and drama. During that time, there were also many _____ discoveries in science. It was one of the most glorious periods in the history of the _____.

T'ang   China
furnish
country   amazing

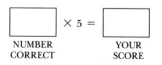

NUMBER
CORRECT

YOUR
SCORE

108

KNOWING HOW TO READ CRITICALLY. Each of the following questions will help you to think critically about the selection. Put an *x* in the box next to the correct answer.

1. Why did Li Tsing sprinkle so many drops of water on the village?
   - ☐ a. He wanted to punish his many enemies there.
   - ☐ b. He believed, mistakenly, that he was rewarding the villagers.
   - ☐ c. His hand slipped and he accidentally poured out half a bottle.

2. When the lady realized that Li had made a terrible blunder, she
   - ☐ a. blamed him for what he had done.
   - ☐ b. punished him for his actions.
   - ☐ c. said it was her fault.

3. When he saw that the flood had drowned everyone in the village, Li must have been
   - ☐ a. saddened and shocked.
   - ☐ b. pleased at his power.
   - ☐ c. relieved that he wasn't in the village at the time.

4. We may infer that if he had asked for the other servant, Li would have bcome a great
   - ☐ a. general anyhow.
   - ☐ b. governor.
   - ☐ c. governor as well as a great general.

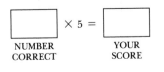

NUMBER CORRECT × 5 = YOUR SCORE

Questions for Writing and Discussion

- Explain how meeting the lady of the house changed Li Tsing's life. Suppose that Li had asked for both servants. What do you think the last sentence of the story would have been?
- The lady of the house was thoughtful and generous. Find evidence from the story to support that statement.
- At the end of the story, Li turned around to look at the house. It had disappeared. How was that possible?

Use the boxes below to total your scores for the exercises. Then write your score on pages 150 and 151.

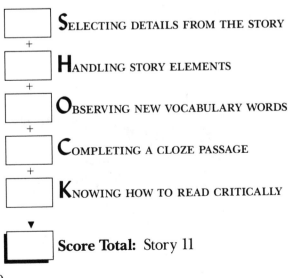

☐ **S**ELECTING DETAILS FROM THE STORY

+

☐ **H**ANDLING STORY ELEMENTS

+

☐ **O**BSERVING NEW VOCABULARY WORDS

+

☐ **C**OMPLETING A CLOZE PASSAGE

+

☐ **K**NOWING HOW TO READ CRITICALLY

▼

☐ **Score Total:** Story 11

12

A Work of Art

BASED ON A STORY
by Anton Chekhov

Sonya Fedorova entered the office of Dr. Koshoff. In her hand she held an object wrapped carefully in newspaper. Her face shone with joy.

"Ah," exclaimed the doctor, "how wonderful to see you. How are you feeling? What is the good news?"

"Doctor," said Sonya, "I have come to thank you. You saved my life. Your skill—your knowledge. Well—I can hardly find words to express myself."

"Say no more," said the doctor, beaming with delight. "I have only done my job. Anyone else would have done the same thing."

"I am poor," said Sonya, "and, as you know, cannot pay you what you really deserve. However, doctor, I beg you to accept a little gift as a **token** of my gratitude."

"Now, now, please—" said the physician.

"No, doctor, you must not refuse," continued Sonya, unfolding her **parcel**. "To do so would **offend** me greatly. What I have brought is a rare work

of art. I have kept it in memory of my father, who was a dealer in antiques. I took over his little shop after he died. The place, I'm sorry to say, is practically falling apart."

She finally succeeded in unwrapping the present and very solemnly placed it on the table.

It was a fairly large candlestick made of bronze. A forest scene was carved around the metal base. It pictured a group of fierce-looking wolves. The animals appeared ready to leap off the bronze.

The doctor looked at the candlestick in silence for several seconds. Then he scratched his head and coughed.

"A beautiful article, to be sure," he said. "A beautiful article, indeed. But I don't think it would be right for me to accept this gift."

"Oh, but you must," said Sonya. "You must."

The doctor scratched his head again. The fact of the matter was that he was deathly afraid of wolves. When he was a child, a village friend had been attacked and killed by a pack of wolves. Since then Koshoff had held them in dread. The very sight of a wolf set his nerves on edge. This candlestick, he knew, would be a very unpleasant reminder.

"I—well—of course, appreciate the thought," said the doctor. "But I can assure you, there's really no need."

"I insist," declared Sonya. "Your refusal would hurt my feelings. After all, you saved my life. I am asking you to accept something I hold very dear. My only regret is that I don't have its companion. As you know, candlesticks come in pairs."

"Thank you very much, then," said Dr. Koshoff. "I can see that there's no use arguing with you."

"No use arguing at all, doctor," replied the grateful patient, very pleased that the doctor was accepting the gift. "What a pity I have just one and not the pair. What a pity, indeed!"

After his caller had departed, the doctor looked closely at his unwelcome gift.

"I suppose," he thought, "it's really a beautiful—an **exquisite**—thing. Still, I can't bear to own it. Let me see, now. To whom shall I give it?"

Then he remembered Vladimir, the lawyer, a friend of his since their

112

school days. Vladimir had recently represented him successfully in a small but very annoying matter.

"Why this is perfect," said the doctor. "As a close friend of mine, he refused to accept a fee. Therefore, it's only right that I give him a present."

Without losing any time, the doctor carefully rewrapped the candlestick and drove to Vladimir's house.

"Hello there, old friend," he said to the lawyer, whom he was happy to find at home. "I have come to thank you for that favor you did for me. You refused to charge me a fee, but you must accept this present as a token of my gratitude. Look—what a beauty!"

On seeing the gift, the lawyer was greatly impressed. "Well, this is quite a work of art. Yes, it's really a gem." Then, having expressed his pleasure, the lawyer went on. "But to tell you the truth, it's not my taste. My style runs to more modern things. It would be a shame to waste this on me. But thank you, anyway."

"Well, this beats everything!" said the doctor. "Just look at this. What a beauty! It fills one with joy merely to see it. Observe the grace, notice the expression. No, I will not have you refuse it. I would feel insulted!"

And with those words the doctor hurried out of the house, glad to be rid of his unwanted gift.

The lawyer studied his present and wondered what to do with it.

"It's really quite attractive, I know," he said, "but I cannot keep it. It goes with nothing here. The thing to do is to give it away. But to whom?"

Suddenly, the answer came to him. His niece, Natasha, was a struggling actress. "She could hardly afford to buy a fine candlestick like this," he thought. Pleased to be able to give Natasha something she would not purchase for herself, the lawyer made up his mind to send it to her at the theater that night.

In the evening, the candlestick, carefully wrapped, was taken by messenger to Natasha's dressing room.

After the performance, Natasha showed it to another actress. "Isn't this a fine work of art?" said Natasha. "Why it must cost a fortune." She paused for a moment, then added, "And here I hardly have enough money to pay this month's rent!"

"Why don't you sell it?" the other suggested. "A neighbor of mine deals in such things. She is very honest and will pay you what it's worth. I'll write down the address."

Natasha agreed.

Two days later Dr. Koshoff was sitting peacefully in his study, thinking of things medical. Suddenly the door of his room flew open, and Sonya Fedorova burst in. Her face beamed with joy, and she was shaking with excitement.

In her hands she held an object wrapped in a newspaper.

"Doctor," she began breathlessly, "imagine my joy! What amazing good luck! I have succeeded in obtaining another candlestick exactly like your own. You now have the pair!"

He opened his mouth and attempted to reply. But words failed him, and he said nothing.

SELECTING DETAILS FROM THE STORY.
Each of the following sentences helps you understand the story. Complete each sentence below by putting an *x* in the box next to the correct answer.

1. Sonya offered Dr. Koshoff a candle-stick because he
   - ☐ a. saved her life.
   - ☐ b. asked her for it.
   - ☐ c. collected works of art.

2. The doctor was not eager to accept the candlestick because it
   - ☐ a. was very ugly.
   - ☐ b. looked so cheap.
   - ☐ c. pictured wolves, which he feared and hated.

3. Dr. Koshoff gave the candlestick to his
   - ☐ a. wife.
   - ☐ b. neice.
   - ☐ c. lawyer.

4. Natasha decided to sell the candlestick in order to
   - ☐ a. get cash for food.
   - ☐ b. obtain money for rent.
   - ☐ c. pay back a loan.

HANDLING STORY ELEMENTS. Each of the following questions reviews your understanding of story elements. Put an *x* in the box next to the correct answer to each question.

1. What happened first in the *plot* of the story?
   - ☐ a. An actress suggested that Natasha sell the candlestick.
   - ☐ b. The lawyer called the candlestick "quite a work of art."
   - ☐ c. Dr. Koshoff said that he didn't think it would be right for him to accept the candlestick.

2. The *mood* of "A Work of Art" is
   - ☐ a. mysterious.
   - ☐ b. humorous.
   - ☐ c. sad.

3. "My style runs to more modern things. It would be a shame to waste this on me." These lines of *dialogue* were spoken by
   - ☐ a. Dr. Koshoff.
   - ☐ b. Vladimir.
   - ☐ c. Natasha.

4. What was the author's *purpose* in writing the story?
   - ☐ a. to entertain the reader
   - ☐ b. to convince the reader
   - ☐ c. to teach the reader an important lesson

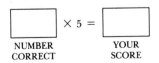

NUMBER
CORRECT

× 5 =

YOUR
SCORE

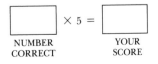

NUMBER
CORRECT

× 5 =

YOUR
SCORE

OBSERVING NEW VOCABULARY WORDS. Answer the following vocabulary questions by putting an *x* in the box next to the correct answer. The vocabulary words are printed in **boldface** in the story. If you wish, look back at the words before you answer the questions.

1. Sonya gave the doctor a little gift as a token of her gratitude. As used here, the word *token* means
   □ a. sign.
   □ b. loss.
   □ c. ticket.

2. She said that refusing the gift would offend her greatly. When you *offend* someone, you
   □ a. make that person happy.
   □ b. offer that person a payment.
   □ c. hurt that person's feelings.

3. The candlestick was really beautiful, an exquisite thing. The word *exquisite* means
   □ a. ordinary.
   □ b. silly.
   □ c. very lovely.

4. She unfolded the parcel and placed it on the table. What is the meaning of the word *parcel*?
   □ a. ribbon
   □ b. package
   □ c. newspaper

COMPLETING A CLOZE PASSAGE. Complete the following paragraph by filling in each blank with one of the words listed in the box below. Each of the words appears in the story. Since there are five words and four blanks, one word in the group will not be used.

Few things are more embarrassing

than having to open a _____
                                1

you don't like in the presence of the giver.

While the other person beams with

_____, you consider what to
        2

say. Then suddenly you _____:
                                    3

It's not the gift that counts; it's the

thought behind it. "Why, it's perfect!" you

exclaim _____.
                4

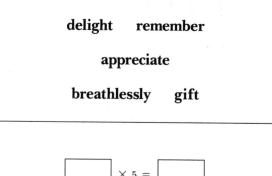

delight   remember

appreciate

breathlessly   gift

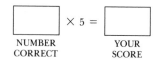

NUMBER
CORRECT

× 5 =

YOUR
SCORE

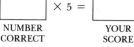

NUMBER
CORRECT

× 5 =

YOUR
SCORE

116

KNOWING HOW TO READ CRITICALLY. Each of the following questions will help you to think critically about the selection. Put an *x* in the box next to the correct answer.

1. How did Sonya get the candlestick she gave to Dr. Koshoff at the end of the story?
   - ☐ a. She found it somewhere in her shop.
   - ☐ b. She bought it at the marketplace.
   - ☐ c. She purchased it from Natasha.

2. We may infer that the second candlestick was
   - ☐ a. even more beautiful than the first one.
   - ☐ b. older and more valuable than the first one.
   - ☐ c. the same one that Sonya gave Dr. Koshoff originally.

3. Which statement is true?
   - ☐ a. Sonya thought that she was doing Dr. Koshoff a favor by giving him the candlesticks.
   - ☐ b. Dr. Koshoff ended up with a pair of candlesticks.
   - ☐ c. Natasha changed her mind and kept the candlestick.

4. When Dr. Koshoff saw the candlestick at the end of the story, he probably felt
   - ☐ a. very amused.
   - ☐ b. disappointed.
   - ☐ c. quite pleased.

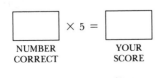

NUMBER CORRECT × 5 = YOUR SCORE

Questions for Writing and Discussion

- Why didn't Dr. Koshoff tell Sonya the truth about the candlestick when she first offered it to him? List as many reasons as you can.
- Sonya thought that finding the "companion" candlestick was "amazing good luck." Was that the case? Explain your answer.
- At the end of the story, Dr. Koshoff once again found himself the owner of the unwanted candlestick. How will he rid himself of the candlestick this time? Be as creative as you like in your answer.

Use the boxes below to total your scores for the exercises. Then write your score on pages 150 and 151.

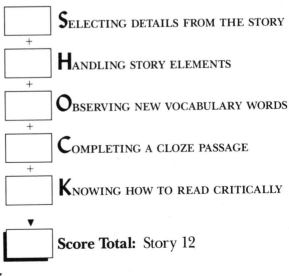

SELECTING DETAILS FROM THE STORY

+

HANDLING STORY ELEMENTS

+

OBSERVING NEW VOCABULARY WORDS

+

COMPLETING A CLOZE PASSAGE

+

KNOWING HOW TO READ CRITICALLY

▼

Score Total: Story 12

13

Mrs. Hinck

by Miriam Allen deFord

Gwen was speaking into the telephone. "I'd like someone to baby-sit," she said. "We've had high school students, but they sometimes invite friends over and play the TV too loud. I think we'd prefer an older person, someone *very* **reliable**. We have two children, a boy eight and a girl five."

Gwen listened while the person at the agency made a suggestion.

"Oh, she sounds fine," said Gwen. "Could she come tomorrow evening at 6:00?"

Mrs. Hinck arrived promptly on the hour. She seemed to be a very pleasant sort of person. The children, Gabe and Ada, seemed to take to her at once. Not only that, Dale wouldn't have to drive Mrs. Hinck home when they got back. She had her own car—a little two-seater—which she parked outside.

"Give the children their supper as soon as we leave," Gwen instructed her. "It's all ready in the kitchen. Ada's bedtime is 8:00 and Gabe can stay up until 9:00. He can take care of himself, but you'll have to help Ada a little."

"Now don't you worry about anything," said Mrs. Hinck. "We're going to get along beautifully."

It was 1:00 A.M. when Gwen and Dale got home. The only light was in the living room where Mrs. Hinck sat knitting. She had even cleaned up the children's supper dishes.

"It's after midnight, so we owe you an hour overtime," Gwen said.

"That's not necessary," replied Mrs. Hinck. "I always stay up late anyway. I'm just knitting here instead of at home."

Gwen and Dale exchanged surprised glances.

"Would you have time to baby-sit here once a week?" Gwen asked. She didn't want to be more definite until she found out how the children had liked Mrs. Hinck. "I'll phone in the morning. What's your number?"

"I'm sorry, but I haven't any phone," said Mrs. Hinck, apologetically. "Just call the agency. I check with them every day."

She folded the wool into a knitting bag, put on her smart black hat and coat, and drove away.

"Well, kids, how were your TV programs last night?" Dale inquired at the breakfast table.

Gabe and Ada stared at each other blankly.

"You know," Gabe said, "we forgot all about them. Mrs. Hinck was telling us a story."

"Do you like her?"

"She's great," they said in chorus.

On Mrs. Hinck's second evening, they arranged for her to come every Saturday.

"And maybe an extra evening once in a while, if you're not too busy," said Gwen.

"Any time," said Mrs. Hinck. "Just let the agency know. To tell the truth, this is all the baby-sitting I'm doing right now. But I'd love to come here whenever you say. I like children, and I get so lonesome for my own little granddaughter, Mary. This is a sweater for her that I'm knitting."

"How old is she?" Gwen asked.

"Just about a year older than your Ada. I miss her a lot."

"Isn't she here in the city?"

"Oh, no, my daughter lives abroad. She married a foreigner. Illinck is his name. I was with them for a while, but I don't know when I'll go back. I do miss Mary and my daughter, too. And Mary misses me. She's an only child, and there are no other children around. I wish Mary had your little boy and girl to play with. They're lovely youngsters."

"We think so," Dale grinned. "Thanks a lot, by the way, for getting them away from all those TV programs. How did you do it?"

"Oh, I just tell them stories," Mrs. Hinck said vaguely. "I guess they just get interested and forget the television. I did the same thing with Mary when I was there. They don't have television, but it was the same thing with the radio."

"Illinck," Dale remarked after Mrs. Hinck had left. "That's a funny name. I wonder what country he's from?"

"I can't imagine. But let's not ask any questions. I noticed she didn't want to discuss that. And we don't want to offend her and lose her—she's so perfect."

After a while, Gwen couldn't avoid feeling a little bit jealous when Gabe and Ada began watching for Mrs. Hinck from the front window. They would rush to the door to greet her with hugs.

"Don't be a goof," Gwen told herself. "She isn't stealing your kids' affection—they're as fond of us as ever."

One day Ada announced, "Whenever Mrs. Hinck goes to visit her grand-daughter, she brings her simply wonderful toys."

"Well, your grandmother brings you toys, too," said Gwen.

"Not like Mrs. Hinck," Ada insisted stubbornly. "Mrs. Hinck brings Mary toys that aren't like any other toys in the world—toys that nobody else in the world has. She told us so."

"I'm getting a bit tired of Mrs. Hinck's little granddaughter," Dale commented to Gwen later. "She must be the worst spoiled brat in the universe."

"Mrs. Hinck does seem kind of wrapped up in the subject, doesn't she?" said Gwen. "But she's just lonely, I guess."

"Toys that aren't like any other toys in the world! That's amazing!"

On another day Gabe said, "When Mrs. Hinck visits her granddaughter she doesn't use a train or a bus or a ship or a plane to get there."

"That's nice. What does she do—walk and swim?"

"No, she just *goes*."

Dale was very curious, but he felt ashamed to be **prying** and changed the subject.

The next time Mrs. Hinck came Gwen asked her, "How's your grand-daughter's sweater coming along?"

"It's almost done. I'm going to make a cap to match. It's for her seventh birthday. Some time this fall I might just pop over and visit there—I do miss Mary so much. How I do wish I could take your two children along! It would be wonderful for Mary."

"Yes, it's too bad it's so far away," Gwen answered. But her heart sank. If Mrs. Hinck left, they would never find another sitter so good. "But you'd come back, wouldn't you?" she asked hopefully.

"Oh, I think so, unless—well, anyway, we don't need to think about it yet."

That was in August. On the first Saturday night in October, Dale and Gwen went to a party. It was after 2:00 when they drove up to their door.

"I feel guilty, keeping Mrs. Hinck up so late," Gwen murmured.

"She's gone to sleep, I guess," Dale said. "There's no light on in the living room."

Gwen let out a startled cry.

"Dale!" she gasped. "Look—her car isn't here. She *couldn't* have gone home and left the children alone in the house—not Mrs. Hinck!"

They raced in. There was no one in the living room or anywhere else on the first floor. Together they ran upstairs, the same sudden terror in their hearts.

The two little bedrooms were dark, and the beds were empty. They had not been slept in.

Dale dashed to the phone to call the police.

"Gwen," he shouted back from the hall, "what's the license number of Mrs. Hinck's car? I never noticed."

"I never did either," said Gwen.

It was almost dawn before the police called back. They'd found the license number from the records and had sent an officer to the address Mrs. Hinck had given as hers. It was an all-night parking lot.

The night attendant there knew Mrs. Hinck by sight, but he hadn't seen her that day. She kept her car there all the time, paying by the month. That was all he knew.

The whole long day was a nightmare. Neither of them had slept, and they kept drinking black coffee to help them stay up. A detective appeared early in the morning and looked at the children's rooms. Nothing of theirs or of their parents' was missing. There were no signs of struggle or any evidence that someone had broken in.

"They were kidnapped, all right," the detective concluded. "But they must have gone willingly."

Gwen told him about Mrs. Hinck's daughter who had married a foreigner named Illinck and lived abroad.

"Never heard of such a name," said the detective. "Is that all you know about him? We'll send out a general alarm right away, of course. But I don't see how she can leave the country without a **passport**." He took out his notebook. "Now give me a full description of your little girl and boy and this Mrs. Hinck."

As the detective was leaving he asked, "You're sure there's no **ransom** note or anything like that?"

"No, nothing at all," said Gwen.

"And there won't be. I'm sure of that," added Dale. "This isn't a kidnapping for money. Mrs. Hinck seemed to be well off. It's more like—well, the way I figure it, she grew fond of our kids and that's why she took them."

"By the way," said the detective, "we've checked with the manager of the agency you got her from. They don't know much about Mrs. Hinck. She just came in there and signed up one day. They sent her out half a dozen times, but she didn't seem to like the people. She wouldn't go back to any of them again—until they sent her to you. And the only address she gave was what turned out to be that parking lot."

"I'm certain," insisted Gwen, "that she's gone to her daughter and grand-daughter and taken Gabe and Ada with her. She told me she might make a visit to them this fall. And she said something, months ago, about wishing she could take our two children along. I thought she was just talking."

"Well," said the detective, "don't lose hope. We ought to have results very soon. From what you've told me, there isn't a chance she'd do any harm to them. And if she makes any attempt to take them out of the country—"

"Oh, *the secret journey*!" said Dale, "I just remembered what Gabe told me yesterday. He said, 'Mrs. Hinck says some day she'll take us on a secret journey to a strange place.' I just laughed. I never thought—"

"The only strange place she's going to see is the inside of a jail," the detective said.

But day passed into night again, and still there was no word. There was a phone call late in the afternoon. It was the detective to say that Mrs. Hinck's car had been found parked in the driveway of a vacant house at the other end of the city.

Husband and wife stood together at the front window where Gabe and Ada had stood so often watching for Mrs. Hinck. They had stood there for a long time, not bothering to turn on the lights in the house as night came on. Dale and Gwen had their arms around each other's shoulders. They stood looking up at the stars.

"Look," Dale said at last, gently, "Are you thinking what I'm thinking?"

Gwen nodded her head slowly.

"I knew you were. Gwen, I studied Latin in school. *Hinc* in Latin means 'on this side,' and *illinc* means 'from that side.' "

Gwen's voice was shaking as she said, "And when Mrs. Hinck goes to visit her granddaughter—"

"She doesn't take a train or a bus or a ship or a plane—she just *goes.*"

"Oh, Dale! There were so many hints that we never even noticed."

"We'd better face it, Gwen. If we're right, the police can't *ever* get them back to us. And Mrs. Hinck won't need any passport where she's taken them!"

Dale paused. Then he added, "Remember what she said, 'I wish Mary had your little boy and girl to play with.' "

"The toys!" Gwen whispered. "The *toys* she was going to bring Mary to play with—the toys that are simply wonderful—the toys that nobody else there has!"

SELECTING DETAILS FROM THE STORY. Each of the following sentences helps you understand the story. Complete each sentence below by putting an *x* in the box next to the correct answer.

1. The children thought that Mrs. Hinck was
   - ☐ a. strange.
   - ☐ b. bossy.
   - ☐ c. great.

2. Mrs. Hinck said that whenever she visited her granddaughter, she brought her
   - ☐ a. clothing from the finest stores.
   - ☐ b. toys that nobody else there had.
   - ☐ c. many interesting games.

3. The detective believed that Mrs. Hinck would
   - ☐ a. come back with the children in a week or two.
   - ☐ b. never be seen or heard from again.
   - ☐ c. be unable to take the children out of the country.

4. At the end of the story, Gwen and Dale realized that Mrs. Hinck had
   - ☐ a. given their boy and girl to Mary.
   - ☐ b. stolen several items from the house.
   - ☐ c. gone to a hiding place not far from their home.

HANDLING STORY ELEMENTS. Each of the following questions reviews your understanding of story elements. Put an *x* in the box next to the correct answer to each question.

1. What is the *setting* of "Mrs. Hinck"?
   - ☐ a. a police station
   - ☐ b. Gwen and Dale's house
   - ☐ c. a distant planet

2. What happened first in the *plot* of the story?
   - ☐ a. Gwen and Dale discovered that their children were missing.
   - ☐ b. Gwen called an agency to hire a baby-sitter.
   - ☐ c. The detective questioned Gwen and Dale.

3. Which expression best *characterizes* Mrs. Hinck?
   - ☐ a. happy as can be
   - ☐ b. just an ordinary person
   - ☐ c. too good to be true

4. Because of the author's *style* of writing, "Mrs. Hinck" is best described as a
   - ☐ a. love story.
   - ☐ b. ghost story.
   - ☐ c. science fiction story.

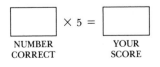

× 5 =

NUMBER CORRECT   YOUR SCORE

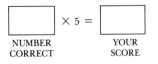

× 5 =

NUMBER CORRECT   YOUR SCORE

OBSERVING NEW VOCABULARY WORDS. Answer the following vocabulary questions by putting an *x* in the box next to the correct answer. The vocabulary words are printed in **boldface** in the story. If you wish, look back at the words before you answer the questions.

1. They wanted an older person to baby-sit—someone very reliable. What is the meaning of the word *reliable*?
   ☐ a. trusty; able to be depended on
   ☐ b. uninteresting; boring or dull
   ☐ c. envious; jealous

2. Dale was very curious about Mrs. Hinck, but he was ashamed to be prying. When you are *prying*, you are
   ☐ a. beginning a difficult puzzle.
   ☐ b. searching with great interest.
   ☐ c. hammering down or beating.

3. The detective asked if the kidnapper had left a ransom note. Which of the following best defines the word *ransom*?
   ☐ a. a message that expresses regret
   ☐ b. a price paid or demanded to set a captive free
   ☐ c. a wish for good luck

4. He said that Mrs. Hinck couldn't leave the country without a passport. What is a *passport*?
   ☐ a. a large sum of money
   ☐ b. a pair of suitcases
   ☐ c. a small book that gives a person permission to travel abroad

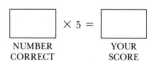

NUMBER CORRECT   × 5 =   YOUR SCORE

COMPLETING A CLOZE PASSAGE. Complete the following paragraph by filling in each blank with one of the words listed in the box below. Each of the words appears in the story. Since there are five words and four blanks, one word in the group will not be used.

Down through the centuries,

_____ have played with toys.
1

There is _____ that dolls
2

made of wood, stone, or cloth existed in

ancient times. In fact, _____
3

shaped like animals were as popular

thousands of years ago as they are today.

Small clay horses, in _____
4

shape, have been found in Egyptian

ruins.

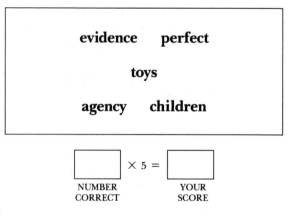

evidence   perfect

toys

agency   children

NUMBER CORRECT   × 5 =   YOUR SCORE

KNOWING HOW TO READ CRITICALLY. Each of the following questions will help you to think critically about the selection. Put an *x* in the box next to the correct answer.

1. We may infer that Mrs. Hinck was
   - ☐ a. an alien, or visitor, from another planet or world.
   - ☐ b. a stranger who was only trying to be helpful.
   - ☐ c. a criminal who spent her life trying to avoid the police.

2. Clues in the story suggest that Ada and Gabe were
   - ☐ a. lost somewhere in their neighborhood.
   - ☐ b. traveling on a bus or train with Mrs. Hinck.
   - ☐ c. the "toys" that Mrs. Hinck was looking for.

3. Mrs. Hinck probably didn't charge Gwen and Dale overtime because she
   - ☐ a. was extremely wealthy.
   - ☐ b. felt very sorry for them.
   - ☐ c. wanted to encourage them to keep using her as a baby-sitter.

4. Which statement is true?
   - ☐ a. Mrs. Hinck kidnapped the children for money.
   - ☐ b. Mrs. Hinck took the children on a secret journey to a strange place.
   - ☐ c. The children went with Mrs. Hinck—but only after a terrible struggle.

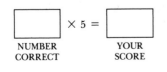

☐ × 5 = ☐

NUMBER CORRECT   YOUR SCORE

Questions for Writing and Discussion

- At the end of the story, Dale and Gwen stood looking up at the stars. Dale gently asked Gwen, "Are you thinking what I'm thinking?" What were Dale and Gwen thinking?
- The detective told Gwen and Dale that Mrs. Hinck baby-sat "half a dozen times, but she didn't seem to like the people. She wouldn't go back to any of them again—until they sent her to you." Explain Mrs. Hinck's actions.
- It is obvious why the story is called "Mrs. Hinck." Think of another fitting and interesting title.

Use the boxes below to total your scores for the exercises. Then write your score on pages 150 and 151.

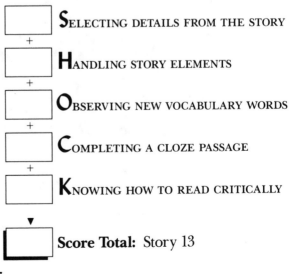

☐ **S**ELECTING DETAILS FROM THE STORY
+
☐ **H**ANDLING STORY ELEMENTS
+
☐ **O**BSERVING NEW VOCABULARY WORDS
+
☐ **C**OMPLETING A CLOZE PASSAGE
+
☐ **K**NOWING HOW TO READ CRITICALLY
▼
☐ **Score Total:** Story 13

14

August Heat

by W. F. Harvey

Phenistone Road, Clapham
August 20, 1906

I have had what is surely the most amazing day in my life. Now, while the events are still fresh in my mind, I wish to write them down here on this paper as clearly as possible.

To begin with, let me say that my name is James Clarence Withencroft.

I am forty years old, in perfect health. I have never been sick a day in my life.

By profession I am an artist. However, I am not a very successful one. Still, I earn enough money by drawing to satisfy my needs, which are rather modest.

My only close relative, a sister, died five years ago, so I have no family.

I ate breakfast this morning at nine o'clock. Then, after looking through the morning paper, I let my mind wander. I was hoping that I might think of some subject to draw.

The room was unbelievably hot, though the door and the windows were open. I had just decided to go to the public swimming pool when an idea for a drawing came to me.

I began to draw what came to mind. So occupied was I with my work, I forgot all about eating lunch. I finally stopped working when the clock struck four.

My drawing, for a hurried sketch, was, I felt sure, the best thing I had ever done.

It showed a criminal in a courtroom right after the judge had announced the sentence. The man was fat—enormously fat. The flesh hung in rolls around his chin. It covered his thick and stumpy chin. He was fairly clean shaven and almost bald. He stood there stiffly, staring straight ahead, while his heavy fingers **clasped** tightly to the rail. There was a look of exhaustion on his face.

I rolled up the sketch. Without really knowing why, I placed it in my pocket. Then I left the house, filled with the sense of pleasure which a thing well done gives.

I believe that I set out with the idea of visiting my friend, Brenton, for I remember walking along Lytton Street. I turned right along Gilcrest Road to the bottom of the hill where there were some workers repairing the road.

From that point on, I have only a vague recollection of where I went. The only thing I really remember was the heat, *the awful heat*. It came up, almost in waves, from the dusty pavement. I longed for the rain promised by the copper-colored clouds that hung low in the sky.

I must have walked five or six miles when a small boy **roused** me from my daydreaming by asking me the time.

I told him it was twenty minutes to seven.

When he left me I looked around to see where I was. I found myself standing in front of a gate that led into a yard. Above the entrance was a sign with the following words:

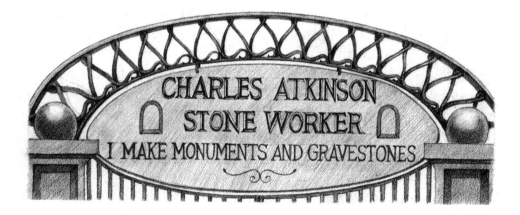

CHARLES ATKINSON
STONE WORKER
I MAKE MONUMENTS AND GRAVESTONES

From inside the yard came a cheerful whistling, the noise of a hammer, and the sharp, cold sound of steel meeting stone.

Something made me enter.

A man was sitting with his back to me, busy at work on a slab of marble. He turned around as he heard my steps. I stopped short.

It was the man I had been drawing! His picture was in my pocket!

He sat there, huge, the sweat pouring from his face which he wiped with a handkerchief. But though the face was the same as the face in my drawing, the expression was quite different.

He greeted me smiling, as if we were old friends. Then he shook my hand.

I apologized for bursting in on him. "Sorry," I said, "but it's so steaming hot and glary outside. This seems like an oasis in the blazing desert."

"Well, I don't know if it's an oasis," he replied, "But it certainly is hot. Take a seat, sir."

He pointed to the end of a large gravestone, and I sat down on it.

"That's a beautiful piece of stone you're working on," I said.

He shook his head slowly. "In a way it is," he answered. "The front of this marble is as smooth and as fine as anything you could want. But there's a thin crack which runs down the back. I could never make a good tombstone out of this piece of marble. It would be all right in the summer, especially in blistering heat like this. But in the winter, the frost would find its way into the crack and would break the stone."

"Then what's this stone for?" I asked.

The man burst out laughing.

"You'll be surprised to hear it's for an exhibition. That's the truth. Artists have exhibitions. Stone workers have them too. The latest little things in tombstones, you know."

He went on talking about his work. He spoke about the different kinds of marble, which stood up best to wind and rain, which were easiest to cut. Then he discussed his garden. Every few minutes he dropped his tools. Then he would wipe his head and complain bitterly about the terrible heat.

I said very little, for I felt uneasy. There was something strange, very strange about meeting this man, this man whose face I had drawn.

I tried, at first, to tell myself that I had seen him somewhere before—that his face had been hidden in a tiny corner of my memory. But I knew that I was just fooling myself.

Mr. Atkinson finished his work. He mopped his **brow** again and got up with a sigh of relief.

"There! Now what do you think of that!" he said proudly.

He pointed at the gravestone. I looked at the words he had carved into the stone. They said—

For some time I sat in silence. A cold **shudder** ran down my spine. Then I asked him, "Where did you see that name?"

"Oh, I didn't see it anywhere," answered Mr. Atkinson. "I needed a name, any name, and I put down the first one that came into my mind. Why do you ask?"

I paused before answering. "It happens to be my name," I said.

He gave a long, low whistle.

"And how about the dates on the stone?"

"I can only tell you about one of them," I said, "—the date of my birth. And that date's correct!"

"That's a strange thing," he said.

But he didn't know the whole story. I explained that I was an artist and told him about my morning's work. Then I took the drawing from my pocket and showed it to him. As he looked at it, the expression on his face changed. It became more and more like that of the man I had drawn.

Then I said, "You probably heard my name some place."

"And you must have seen me somewhere and have forgotten it. Did you ever go on vacation at Clacton?"

I had never been to Clacton in my life. We were silent for a long time. We were both looking at the same thing. There were two dates on the gravestone. And the first one was right!

"Come inside and have supper," said Mr. Atkinson.

He introduced me to his wife as a friend who was an artist. After an excellent meal, she and I spent half an hour or so in conversation. Then I went outside and found Atkinson sitting on the gravestone.

We continued our conversation at the point we had left off.

I said, "You must excuse me for asking, but have you done anything for which you could be put on trial?"

He shook his head and said, "No." Then he got up, took a can from the porch, and began to water the flowers. It certainly was hot. "Where do you live?" he asked.

I told him my address. Even walking quickly, it would take me an hour to get home.

"Look," he said, "let's consider this intelligently. Think about that second date on the tombstone! If you leave for home now, you could have an accident. You might get run over. You could have a bad fall. Anything could happen."

He mentioned other unlikely things, things I would have laughed at earlier in the day. I did not laugh now!

"The best thing to do," he went on, "is for you to stay here until twelve o'clock. Why don't we go upstairs and relax? It may be cooler inside."

To my surprise I agreed.

We are now sitting in a small room on the second floor. Atkinson's wife has gone to bed. He is busy sharpening some tools.

The air seems charged with thunder. It is blazing hot. I am writing these words on a shaky table in front of the open window. The leg of the table is cracked. Atkinson, who is a handy man with tools, is going to fix it as soon as he has finished sharpening his chisel.

It is after eleven o'clock now. I shall be gone in less than an hour.

But the heat is unbearable. It is truly unbearable.

It is enough to make a man mad!

SELECTING DETAILS FROM THE STORY.
Each of the following sentences helps you understand the story. Complete each sentence below by putting an *x* in the box next to the correct answer.

1. James Clarence Withencroft's drawing showed
   - ☐ a. people swimming in a pool.
   - ☐ b. a criminal in a courtroom.
   - ☐ c. a man sitting on a gravestone.

2. When he looked at Charles Atkinson, Withencroft was surprised to discover that
   - ☐ a. he had once met Atkinson on a vacation at Clacton.
   - ☐ b. he had gone to school with Atkinson years ago.
   - ☐ c. Atkinson was the man he had been drawing earlier.

3. The words carved into the gravestone gave
   - ☐ a. the dates of Withencroft's birth and death.
   - ☐ b. Withencroft's address and occupation.
   - ☐ c. the name of the man who carved the stone.

4. At the end of the story, Withencroft decided to
   - ☐ a. go home at once.
   - ☐ b. hide in the stone yard all night.
   - ☐ c. wait at Atkinson's house until midnight.

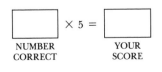

NUMBER CORRECT × 5 = YOUR SCORE

HANDLING STORY ELEMENTS. Each of the following questions reviews your understanding of story elements. Put an *x* in the box next to the correct answer to each question.

1. What happened last in the *plot* of "August Heat"?
   - ☐ a. Withencroft waited for Atkinson to return with a chisel.
   - ☐ b. Withencroft had supper with Atkinson and his wife.
   - ☐ c. Withencroft found himself in front of a gate that led into a yard.

2. The story is *set*
   - ☐ a. on a steaming hot August day in 1906.
   - ☐ b. in a graveyard at the present time.
   - ☐ c. in a house in the country a few years ago.

3. "If you leave for home now, you could have an accident." That line of *dialogue* was spoken by
   - ☐ a. Withencroft.
   - ☐ b. Atkinson.
   - ☐ c. Atkinson's wife.

4. The *mood* of "August Heat" is
   - ☐ a. light and amusing.
   - ☐ b. suspenseful.
   - ☐ c. humorous.

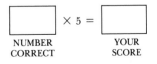

NUMBER CORRECT × 5 = YOUR SCORE

OBSERVING NEW VOCABULARY WORDS. Answer the following vocabulary questions by putting an *x* in the box next to the correct answer. The vocabulary words are printed in **boldface** in the story. If you wish, look back at the words before you answer the questions.

1. The man's heavy fingers clasped tightly to the rail. What is the meaning of the word *clasped*?
   - ☐ a. grasped
   - ☐ b. slipped
   - ☐ c. bounced

2. He walked five or six miles when a small boy roused him from his daydreaming. The word *roused* means
   - ☐ a. relaxed.
   - ☐ b. woke up.
   - ☐ c. struck.

3. Atkinson complained bitterly about the heat, then mopped his brow. Define the word *brow*.
   - ☐ a. forehead
   - ☐ b. floor
   - ☐ c. tools

4. When Withencroft saw what was written on the tombstone, a cold shudder ran down his spine. As used here, the word *shudder* means
   - ☐ a. breeze.
   - ☐ b. shirt.
   - ☐ c. trembling.

COMPLETING A CLOZE PASSAGE. Complete the following paragraph by filling in each blank with one of the words listed in the box below. Each of the words appears in the story. Since there are five words and four blanks, one word in the group will not be used.

It is interesting to _____ how the months got their names.

The month of July, for example, is _____ after *Julius* Caesar. It is not _____, however, if Caesar named the month for himself or if the Roman Senate paid him this honor. The month of _____ is named after Emperor *Augustus*, the first Roman emperor.

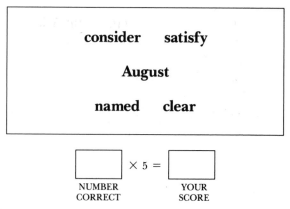

consider	satisfy
August	
named	**clear**

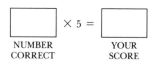

× 5 =

NUMBER CORRECT   YOUR SCORE

× 5 =

NUMBER CORRECT   YOUR SCORE

KNOWING HOW TO READ CRITICALLY. Each of the following questions will help you to think critically about the selection. Put an *x* in the box next to the correct answer.

1. Clues in the story suggest that Atkinson eventually
   - ☐ a. said goodbye to Withencroft and watched him leave.
   - ☐ b. became one of Withencroft's best friends.
   - ☐ c. killed Withencroft with a sharp chisel.

2. We may infer that Withencroft
   - ☐ a. arrived home safely around one o'clock in the morning.
   - ☐ b. died between eleven and twelve o'clock that night.
   - ☐ c. spent another day at Atkinson's house, then went home.

3. Which statement is true?
   - ☐ a. Withencroft was a very successful and well-known artist.
   - ☐ b. Withencroft was certain that he had seen Atkinson before.
   - ☐ c. The heat probably drove Atkinson mad.

4. Hints in the story suggest that Atkinson
   - ☐ a. was put on trial for Withencroft's death.
   - ☐ b. had nothing to do with Withencroft's death.
   - ☐ c. was not a very good stone worker.

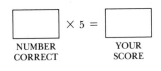

NUMBER CORRECT   × 5 =   YOUR SCORE

Questions for Writing and Discussion

- Why did Atkinson suggest that Withencroft stay at his house until twelve o'clock? Suppose that Withencroft had started off for his home at once. What do you think would have happened? Use your imagination. Hint: involve Atkinson.
- After eleven o'clock Withencroft said, "I shall be gone in less than an hour." Explain how that statement has at least two meanings.
- Read the last three lines of the story again. Fully explain their importance.

Use the boxes below to total your scores for the exercises. Then write your score on pages 150 and 151.

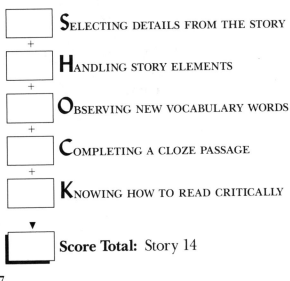

☐ **S**ELECTING DETAILS FROM THE STORY
+
☐ **H**ANDLING STORY ELEMENTS
+
☐ **O**BSERVING NEW VOCABULARY WORDS
+
☐ **C**OMPLETING A CLOZE PASSAGE
+
☐ **K**NOWING HOW TO READ CRITICALLY
▼
☐ **Score Total:** Story 14

15

The Flying Machine

by Ray Bradbury

In the year A.D. 400, the Emperor Yuan held his throne by the Great Wall of China, and the land was green with rain, readying itself toward the harvest, at peace, the people in his dominion[1] neither too happy nor too sad.

Early on the morning of the first day of the first week of the second month of the new year, the Emperor Yuan was sipping tea and fanning himself against a warm breeze when a servant ran across the scarlet and blue garden tiles, calling, "Oh, Emperor, a miracle!"

"Yes," said the emperor, "the air *is* sweet this morning."

"No, no, a miracle!" said the servant, bowing quickly.

"And this tea is good in my mouth, surely that is a miracle."

"No, no, Your Excellency."

"Let me guess then—the sun has risen and a new day is upon us. Or the sea is blue. *That,* now, is the finest of all miracles."

"Excellency, a man is flying!"

"What?" The emperor stopped his fan.

"I saw him in the air, a man flying with wings. I heard a voice call out of the sky, and when I looked up, there he was, a dragon in the heavens with

---

1. **dominion:** country or territory.

a man in its mouth, a dragon of paper and bamboo, colored like the sun and the grass."

"It is early," said the emperor, "and you have just wakened from a dream."

"It is early, but I have seen what I have seen! Come, and you will see it too."

"Sit down with me here," said the emperor. "Drink some tea. It must be a strange thing, if it is true, to see a man fly. You must have time to think of it, even as I must have time to prepare myself for the sight."

They drank tea.

"Please," said the servant at last, "or he will be gone."

The emperor rose thoughtfully. "Now you may show me what you have seen."

They walked into a garden, across a meadow of grass, over a small bridge, through a grove of trees, and up a tiny hill.

"There!" said the servant.

The emperor looked into the sky.

And in the sky, laughing so high that you could hardly hear him laugh, was a man; and the man was clothed in bright papers and reeds to make wings and a beautiful yellow tail, and he was soaring all about like the largest bird in a universe of birds, like a new dragon in a land of ancient dragons.

The man called down to them from high in the cool winds of morning, "I fly, I fly!"

The servant waved to him. "Yes, yes!"

The Emperor Yuan did not move. Instead he looked at the Great Wall of China now taking shape out of the farthest mist in the green hills, that splendid snake of stones which **writhed** with majesty across the entire land. That wonderful wall which had protected them for a timeless time from enemy hordes and preserved peace for years without number. He saw the town, **nestled** to itself by a river and a road and a hill, beginning to waken.

"Tell me," he said to his servant, "has anyone else seen this flying man?"

"I am the only one, Excellency," said the servant, smiling at the sky, waving.

The emperor watched the heavens another minute and then said, "Call him down to me."

"Ho, come down, come down! The emperor wishes to see you!" called the servant, hands cupped to his shouting mouth.

The emperor glanced in all directions while the flying man soared down the morning wind. He saw a farmer, early in his fields, watching the sky, and he noted where the farmer stood.

The flying man alighted with a rustle of paper and a creak of bamboo reeds. He came proudly to the emperor, clumsy in his rig, at last bowing before the old man.

"What have you done?" demanded the emperor.

"I have flown in the sky, Your Excellency," replied the man.

"What *have* you done?" said the emperor again.

"I have just told you!" cried the flier.

"You have told me nothing at all." The emperor reached out a thin hand to touch the pretty paper and the birdlike keel of the **apparatus**. It smelled cool, of the wind.

"Is it not beautiful, Excellency?"

"Yes, too beautiful."

"It is the only one in the world!" smiled the man. "And I am the inventor."

"The *only* one in the world?"

"I swear it!"

"Who else knows of this?"

"No one. Not even my wife, who would think me mad with the sun. She thought I was making a kite. I rose in the night and walked to the cliffs far away. And when the morning breezes blew and the sun rose, I gathered my courage, Excellency, and leaped from the cliff. I flew! But my wife does not know of it."

"Well for her, then," said the emperor. "Come along."

They walked back to the great house. The sun was full in the sky now, and the smell of the grass was refreshing. The emperor, the servant, and the flier paused within the huge garden.

The emperor clapped his hands. "Ho, guards!"

The guards came running.

"Hold this man."

The guards seized the flier.

"Call the executioner," said the emperor.

"What's this!" cried the flier, bewildered. "What have I done?" He began to weep, so that the beautiful paper apparatus rustled.

"Here is the man who has made a certain machine," said the emperor, "and yet asks us what he has created. He does not know himself. It is only necessary that he create, without knowing why he has done so, or what this thing will do."

The executioner came running with a sharp silver ax. He stood with his naked, large-muscled arms ready, his face covered with a serene white mask.

"One moment," said the emperor. He turned to a nearby table upon which sat a machine that he himself had created. The emperor took a tiny golden key from his own neck. He fitted this key to the tiny, delicate machine and wound it up. Then he set the machine going.

The machine was a garden of metal and jewels. Set in motion, birds sang in tiny metal trees, wolves walked through a miniature forest, and tiny people ran in and out of sun and shadow, fanning themselves with miniature fans, listening to the tiny emerald birds, and standing by impossibly small but tinkling fountains.

"Is *it* not beautiful?" said the emperor. "If you asked me what I have done here, I could answer you well. I have made birds sing, I have made forests murmur, I have set people to walking in this woodland, enjoying the leaves and shadows and songs. That is what I have done."

"But, oh, Emperor!" pleaded the flier, on his knees, the tears pouring down his face. "I have done a similar thing! I have found beauty. I have flown on the morning wind. I have looked down on all the sleeping houses and gardens. I have smelled the sea and even *seen* it, beyond the hills, from my high place. And I have soared like a bird; oh, I cannot say how beautiful it is up there, in the sky, with the wind about me, the wind blowing me here like a feather, there like a fan, the way the sky smells in the morning! And how free one feels! *That* is beautiful, Emperor, that is beautiful, too!"

"Yes," said the emperor sadly, "I know it must be true. For I felt my heart move with you in the air and I wondered: What is it like? How does it feel? How do the distant pools look from so high? And how my houses and servants? Like ants? And how the distant towns not yet awake?"

"Then spare me!"

"But there are times," said the emperor, more sadly still, "when one must lose a little beauty if one is to keep what little beauty one already has. I do not fear you, yourself, but I fear another man."

"What man?"

"Some other man who, seeing you, will build a thing of bright papers and bamboo like this. But the other man will have an evil face and an evil heart, and the beauty will be gone. It is this man I fear."

"Why? Why?"

"Who is to say that someday just such a man, in just such an apparatus of paper and reed, might not fly in the sky and drop huge stones upon the Great Wall of China?" said the emperor.

No one moved or said a word.

"Off with his head," said the emperor.

The executioner whirled his silver ax.

"Burn the kite and the inventor's body and bury their ashes together," said the emperor.

The servants retreated to obey.

The emperor turned to his hand servant, who had seen the man flying. "Hold your tongue. It was all a dream, a most sorrowful and beautiful dream.

And that farmer in the distant field who also saw, tell him it would pay him to consider it only a vision. If ever the word passes around, you and the farmer die within the hour."

"You are merciful, Emperor."

"No, not merciful," said the old man. Beyond the garden wall he saw the guard burning the beautiful machine of paper and reeds that smelled of the morning wind. He saw the dark smoke climb into the sky. "No, only very much bewildered and afraid." He saw the guards digging a tiny pit wherein to bury the ashes. "What is the life of one man against those of a million others? I must take solace[2] from that thought."

He took the key from its chain about his neck and once more wound up the beautiful miniature garden. He stood looking out across the land at the Great Wall, the peaceful town, the green fields, the rivers and streams. He sighed. The tiny garden whirred its hidden and delicate machinery and set itself in motion; tiny people walked in the forest, tiny foxes loped through sun-speckled **glades** in beautiful shining pelts, and among the tiny trees flew little bits of high song and bright blue and yellow color, flying, flying, flying in that small sky.

"Oh," said the emperor, closing his eyes, "look at the birds, look at the birds!"

---

2. **solace:** comfort or relief.

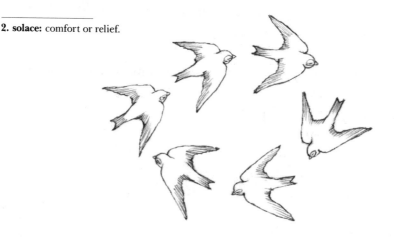

SELECTING DETAILS FROM THE STORY.
Each of the following sentences helps you understand the story. Complete each sentence below by putting an *x* in the box next to the correct answer.

1. A servant told the emperor that he had seen a man
   - [ ] a. chipping stones from the Great Wall of China.
   - [ ] b. attempting to break into the palace.
   - [ ] c. flying with wings.

2. Emperor Yuan asked the flier
   - [ ] a. when he thought of his invention.
   - [ ] b. who else knew of his invention.
   - [ ] c. how much money he wanted for his invention.

3. The emperor ordered that the flier be
   - [ ] a. killed.
   - [ ] b. rewarded.
   - [ ] c. hidden.

4. The emperor was afraid that some other man would
   - [ ] a. see the invention and destroy it.
   - [ ] b. claim that the invention had been stolen from him.
   - [ ] c. build a similar invention and use it for evil purposes.

HANDLING STORY ELEMENTS. Each of the following questions reviews your understanding of story elements. Put an *x* in the box next to the correct answer to each question.

1. What happened first in the *plot* of "The Flying Machine"?
   - [ ] a. The emperor called for the executioner.
   - [ ] b. The servant cupped his hands and called for the flier to come down.
   - [ ] c. The emperor took a key from his neck and wound up his mechanical garden.

2. Who is the *main character* in the story?
   - [ ] a. the flier
   - [ ] b. the Emperor Yuan
   - [ ] c. the servant

3. "The Flying Machine" is *set* in
   - [ ] a. China in the year A.D. 400.
   - [ ] b. Japan at the present time.
   - [ ] c. India many years ago.

4. Which sentence best tells the *theme* of the story?
   - [ ] a. An inventor pleads with an emperor for mercy.
   - [ ] b. A man figures out how to fly by inventing a machine made of bamboo and paper.
   - [ ] c. When an emperor fears how an invention may be used, he destroys the inventor and his beautiful invention.

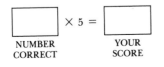

NUMBER CORRECT × 5 = YOUR SCORE

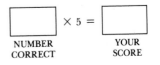

NUMBER CORRECT × 5 = YOUR SCORE

OBSERVING NEW VOCABULARY WORDS.
Answer the following vocabulary questions by putting an *x* in the box next to the correct answer. The vocabulary words are printed in **boldface** in the story. If you wish, look back at the words before you answer the questions.

1. The emperor reached out to touch the apparatus that the man had been flying. As used here, the word *apparatus* means
   □ a. gift.
   □ b. gust of wind.
   □ c. machine.

2. The Great Wall of China, a snake of stones, writhed across the entire land. The word *writhed* means
   □ a. twisted and turned.
   □ b. fell apart.
   □ c. hissed at.

3. Tiny people walked in the forest, and tiny foxes loped through the glades. What are *glades*?
   □ a. open spaces in a forest
   □ b. avenues or highways
   □ c. shops or stores

4. The Emperor Yuan saw the town, nestled by a river and a road and a hill. What is the meaning of the word *nestled*?
   □ a. destroyed
   □ b. settled cozily
   □ c. rushing by noisily

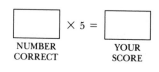

NUMBER CORRECT × 5 = YOUR SCORE

COMPLETING A CLOZE PASSAGE. Complete the following paragraph by filling in each blank with one of the words listed in the box below. Each of the words appears in the story. Since there are five words and four blanks, one word in the group will not be used.

Although _____ are usually

flown for pleasure, they have serious uses,

too. More than two thousand years ago,

a Chinese general _____

the kite to use in war. For a hundred

_____ , kites have been used

to measure the weather. Do you remember

the story about Ben Franklin's famous

experiment? He _____ a kite to

prove that natural lightning is electricity.

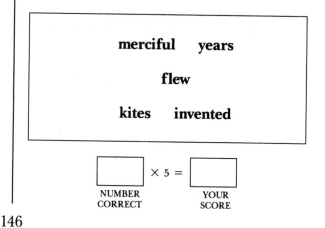

merciful   years

flew

kites   invented

NUMBER CORRECT × 5 = YOUR SCORE

KNOWING HOW TO READ CRITICALLY. Each of the following questions will help you to think critically about the selection. Put an *x* in the box next to the correct answer.

1. Which statement is true?
   - ☐ a. The emperor thought the invention was beautiful—but he feared it.
   - ☐ b. The emperor put to death the farmer who saw the man flying.
   - ☐ c. The emperor was used to seeing the man fly.

2. If the flier's wife had known about the invention, the emperor may have
   - ☐ a. sent her out of the country.
   - ☐ b. ordered that she be killed.
   - ☐ c. asked her how the invention was made.

3. When he showed the Emperor Yuan his invention, the flier probably thought that the emperor would be
   - ☐ a. pleased.
   - ☐ b. troubled.
   - ☐ c. angry.

4. When the emperor asked, "What is the life of one man against those of a million others?" he meant it was
   - ☐ a. silly for one person to try to fight a huge crowd.
   - ☐ b. very unlikely that someone would think of a great invention.
   - ☐ c. necessary to sacrifice one person to protect many others.

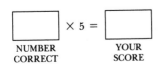

NUMBER CORRECT × 5 = YOUR SCORE

Questions for Writing and Discussion
- Why did the Emperor Yuan decide to have the inventor put to death? What else might the emperor have done? Explain why you agree or disagree with the emperor's decision.
- Compare the emperor's mechanical garden with the flier's invention. In what ways are they similar? How are they different?
- The emperor said, "There are times when one must lose a little beauty if one is to keep what little beauty one already has." Explain what the emperor meant by that statement. Do you agree with him? Why?

Use the boxes below to total your scores for the exercises. Then write your score on pages 150 and 151.

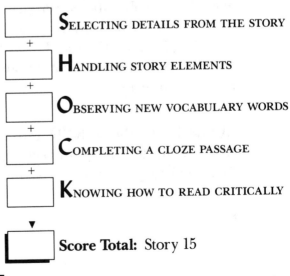

SELECTING DETAILS FROM THE STORY

+

HANDLING STORY ELEMENTS

+

OBSERVING NEW VOCABULARY WORDS

+

COMPLETING A CLOZE PASSAGE

+

KNOWING HOW TO READ CRITICALLY

▼

Score Total: Story 15

Acknowledgments

Acknowledgment is gratefully made to the following publishers, authors, and agents for permission to reprint these works. Adaptations and abridgments are by Burton Goodman.

"The Jigsaw Puzzle" by Judith Bauer Stamper. From *Tales from the Midnight Hour* © by Judith Bauer Stamper. Used by permission of Scholastic, Inc.

"The Eyes Have It" by James McKimmey. Renewal of ©1981 by James McKimmey. Reprinted by permission of James McKimmey.

"The Bus (adaptation)," ©1965 by Stanley Edgar Hyman, adaptation, from *Come Along with Me* by Shirley Jackson. Used by permission of Viking Penguin, a division of Penguin Books USA Inc.

"Otero's Visitor" by Manuela Williams Crosno. ©1987 by Manuela Williams Crosno. Reprinted by permission of Manuela Williams Crosno.

"Anansi's Fishing Trip" A Tale from Ghana. The Faith Press Ltd., England and Drum Publications (Proprietary) Ltd., Johannesburgh: "Anansi's Fishing Trip" from *African Voices: An Anthology of Native African Writing*, edited by Peggy Rutherfoord. All attempts have been made to locate The Faith Press Ltd., Drum Publications Ltd., and the copyright holder, but no clear records exist.

"A Lodging for the Night" by Lin Yutang. From *Famous Chinese Short Stories* ©1948, 1951, 1952 by (John Day Company) Harper & Row, Publishers, Inc. Reprinted by permission of Hsiang Ju Lin for The Estate of Lin Yutang.

Progress Chart

1. Write in your score for each exercise.
2. Write in your Score Total.

	S	H	O	C	K	SCORE TOTAL
Story 1						
Story 2						
Story 3						
Story 4						
Story 5						
Story 6						
Story 7						
Story 8						
Story 9						
Story 10						
Story 11						
Story 12						
Story 13						
Story 14						
Story 15						

Progress Graph

1. Write your Score Total in the box under the number for each story.
2. Put an *x* along the line above each box to show your Score Total for that story.
3. Make a graph of your progress by drawing a line to connect the *x*'s.

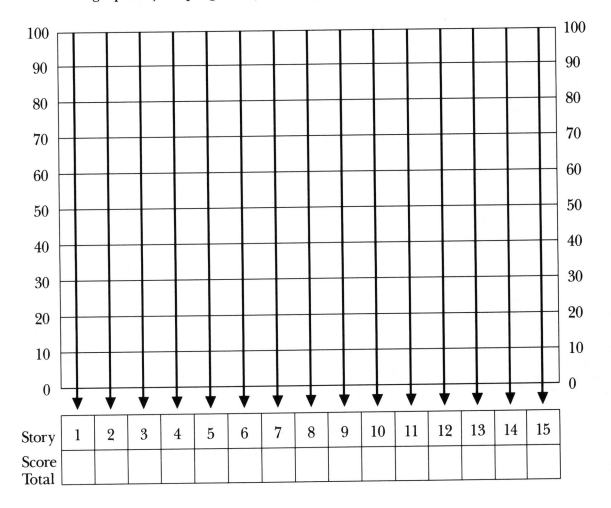